T0283898

# WHY
# MARIAH
# CAREY
# MATTERS

Music
Matters

Evelyn McDonnell and Oliver Wang

*Series Editors*

BOOKS IN THE SERIES

# WHY MARIAH CAREY MATTERS

Andrew Chan

UNIVERSITY OF TEXAS PRESS

AUSTIN

Requests for permission to reproduce material from this work should be sent to:
    Permissions
    University of Texas Press
    P.O. Box 7819
    Austin, TX 78713-7819
    utpress.utexas.edu

♾ The paper used in this book meets the minimum requirements of ANSI/NISO Z39.48-1992 (R1997) (Permanence of Paper).

Library of Congress Cataloging-in-Publication Data

Names: Chan, Andrew, 1986– author.
Title: Why Mariah Carey matters / Andrew Chan.
Other titles: Music matters.
Description: First edition. | Austin : University of Texas Press, 2023. | Series: Music matters | Includes bibliographical references.
Identifiers: LCCN 2022062218 (print) | LCCN 2022062219 (ebook)
    ISBN 978-1-4773-2507-0 (hardcover)
    ISBN 978-1-4773-2508-7 (pdf)
    ISBN 978-1-4773-2509-4 (epub)
Subjects: LCSH: Carey, Mariah. | Carey, Mariah—Criticism and interpretation. | Women singers—United States—Biography. | Women lyricists—United States—Biography. | Popular music—United States—History and criticism. | Music and race—United States—History. | LCGFT: Biographies.
Classification: LCC ML420.C2555 C53 2023 (print) | LCC ML420.C2555 (ebook) | DDC 782.42164092 [B]—dc23/eng/20230117
LC record available at https://lccn.loc.gov/2022062218
LC ebook record available at https://lccn.loc.gov/2022062219

doi:10.7560/325070

For Goeun,
my sister in song

# CONTENTS

# A CALL TO WORSHIP

When I was a child, I had a dream about living inside a singer's voice box. I couldn't explain this surreal vision, but I think it was a way of getting my head around something that's obvious to me now: that the singing that moves me most deeply, the kind that could make me cry even when I was too young to understand the words being sung, engages far more than just my ears.

Singers are always working (intentionally or not) at the level of texture and shape, which means that the sensations they evoke in us are not simply aural but tactile. A few seconds into a performance, I might feel as if I've been caressed by a breeze, or wrapped in velvet, or sliced open by a surgeon's blade. True virtuosos are aware of this power and are never content to just be heard; they create sonic environments and bid us enter with our whole bodies. The most ambitious among them treat the voice as a kind of palace, each note a room to be inhabited, each timbral effect a surface inviting us to touch.

Absurd or overwrought as they may seem, such metaphors are hard to avoid when contemplating great voices. How else to describe the outsize effect of an instrument as banal as life itself, a sound produced by two slender pieces of tissue stretched across the opening of the trachea?

To pin these metaphors down to something rational,

some listeners lean on quantitative or taxonomic methods. A few years ago, I stumbled down a rabbit hole of fan-made YouTube videos that analyze various aspects of Mariah Carey's singing. I was transfixed. The more esoterically technical the approach, the more excited I got. And of course, the more I watched, the more of these videos surfaced, until it seemed I was being immersed in the cryptic language of an underground cult.

I watched for what must have been hours. One video compiled every pitch in Mariah's five-octave range (sixty-five in total), ascending from her leathery lows to her birdlike highs in one minute, unbroken by breaths. In another, a music professor tried to determine Mariah's *Fach*, employing an old German system originally designed to categorize classical singers. Elsewhere, amateurs deconstructed Mariah's trademark melismata, tallying the number of notes she could cram into however many seconds. Other videos compared studio and live versions of her best-known songs, toggling between footage from multiple decades to detect the minutest variations in resonance, tone, and diaphragmatic support. In the comments, superfans expressed their preference for how Mariah had finessed a certain phrase on *Arsenio Hall* in 1990 or at the Tokyo Dome in 1996, or made a contrarian argument for a concert from the early 2000s available only in a blurry, digitized bootleg.

These people are obsessed, I thought. This is idol worship gone too far. But there was something touching about this urge to collect the queen's every utterance, the way a literary archivist might preserve a writer's discarded drafts. I guess I knew, deep down, that I was one of them.

It's been a while since I've watched those videos, but

they've since become a bona fide genre on the internet — scrappy, homemade content that, to some modest extent, demystifies the most enigmatic of performing arts. As a lifelong diva lover with no solid musical training to speak of, I absorbed the videos' teachings like coursework. I still remember many of the perfectly useless factoids in them, and in my mind's ear I can call forth Mariah's belted E5s and F5s — those radiant money notes — despite not being gifted with absolute pitch.

One thing the videos affirmed for me is that voices can seduce us, haunt us, heal us regardless of the text they're delivering or even the culture that surrounds them. Of course, it's the text that brings the voice to the masses, and it's the culture that teaches the voice its steps, that gives it space to signify and reverberate. (What would Mariah sound like if she'd been raised, say, during the Song Dynasty or at the height of the Italian Renaissance?) But a voice also carries something ineffable in its very grain, and in its individuality, we hear something profound.

At the mercy of the superfans' slicing and dicing, reconstituted in the form of isolated notes and phrases, Mariah's voice could be experienced as a natural phenomenon, worthy of ecstatic contemplation. Hearing it decoupled from context was as good a way as any of getting closer to it, of pressing my ear against it. The question of what about it demands (and rewards) such attentive listening may never be adequately answered. But the curiosity fueling the question, implicit in all those videos, is where the pleasure lies.

Taking such exacting measurements of a voice has its pitfalls, though, one of them being the further abstraction and disembodiment of that voice, which, once we consume it, has already been separated from its human source by time, distance, and the manipulations and distortions of recording technology. A voice can be so gigantic, so opulently decked out, that it overshadows the mind operating it. Pop history assumes such a voice needs to be tamed and trained by someone more judicious than the star herself— usually a man. Cases in point: Whitney Houston, who was advised by record executive Clive Davis to not write her own songs; and Aretha Franklin, who supposedly benefited from producer Jerry Wexler unlocking her authentic self. It's telling that the most enduring pop-culture representations of singing ingenues — *The Phantom of the Opera*, *The Little Mermaid*—envision the voice as a detachable organ, one that can fall into the hands of a Svengali or be siphoned right out of the woman's throat.

Maybe so many serious music lovers find virtuoso pop singers distasteful because they assume that a beautiful voice is something someone is just born with, like physical attractiveness. Based on this logic, to make a spectacle out of one's voice is to commit an act of vanity unrelated to the noble aims of art. Such disdain goes hand in hand with the widespread underestimation of singers' creative agency, and it has dogged many pop divas, including those who made it big in the '90s, when extravagant female voices reached peak profitability. It's this disdain to which those YouTube fan videos form a pointed, resounding rebuttal.

Despite her record-breaking triumphs (including nineteen chart-topping singles, more than any solo artist in history) and a tenaciously loyal, multigenerational fanbase (known affectionately as "lambs"), Mariah continues to epitomize the perennial diva's dilemma. Questions of her credibility emerged almost as soon as she made her debut in the spring of 1990. Most obviously, there was the pervasive sense of a conflict of interest. If she was so firmly tucked under the wing of Sony CEO Tommy Mottola—who spotted her at a party in a Cinderella moment that strained credulity, and with whom she ended up sharing a turbulent marriage from 1993 to 1998—could she be trusted to possess any real musicianship? And weren't her immediate blockbuster sales just the foregone conclusion of a rigged game? The longevity of these questions might partially explain why there has been no book-length critical appreciation of her work until now.

Thanks to the obvious bloat of an industry sustained by exorbitant budgets, hyper-produced stadium tours and videos, and the swift conglomeration of record labels that occurred in the 1980s, it was natural for audiences to feel as if they were being force-fed ready-made superstars. Nothing about Mariah's rise looked organic; to cynical eyes, her assembly line–like productivity throughout the '90s (and the steady stream of Number 1 hits that flowed from it) must have seemed the result of a pact with the devil. Mariah's own account of those years paints a similar picture: she has said that her husband-overlord forced her into conservative turtlenecks, found every possible way of dimming her personality, and kept her inaccessible to her friends, family, and public—all while milking her for middle-of-the-road hits.

If the misogyny at play was identifiable from the beginning, the racial dynamics took several more years to garner widespread awareness. Though Mariah was born to a Black and Venezuelan American father and an Irish American mother, the *Los Angeles Times* reported on multiple occasions in 1990 and 1991 that the singer was white.[1] In an age when the once racially specific aesthetics of soul and gospel were being appropriated into the white-friendly precincts of mainstream pop—inflaming long-standing anguish over the systemic underacknowledgment of Black musicians—counterfactual remarks like these could seep into the cultural bloodstream and linger there.

The experience of not being taken seriously has been central to Mariah's persona, repeatedly casting her as an underdog. But the notion of Mariah as a puppet need not have gained as much traction as it did. Her early TV appearances introduced her as a young, soft-spoken artist calmly asserting herself as the principal force behind her work to anyone who would listen. Barely out of her teens, she was already describing herself as a songwriter and producer. There's a YouTube supercut of her insistently claiming this credit over the years, sometimes with a laugh tinged with undisguised bitterness. Almost as frequently, she explained her mixed-race identity, which should have killed any idea that she ever tried to conceal it for commercial advantage.

Speculation that her voice was little more than a studio invention may have been understandable considering the fallout from the Milli Vanilli lip-syncing scandal in 1989. But all doubts should have been laid to rest by Mariah's first years of TV performances, not just because of the undeniable talent they showcase but because of the stray imperfections that corroborate the liveness of the singing, signs of a newcomer intent on proving her chops even at the risk of overreaching. Her first several performances of "Vision of Love," the stately, gospel-inflected single that announced her arrival, run the gamut in taste and effectiveness. On *Good Morning America*, she prefaces the song with an impressive but overbearing demonstration of ability, warming up with fluttery whistle tones and a cavernous bellow from deep in her chest. On *Saturday Night Live*, the famously showboating climax — built on a series of loops around the word "all" that inspired critic Sasha Frere-Jones to call the song "the Magna Carta of melisma"[2] — goes ever so slightly off the rails with a few too many extra curlicues. Mariah's gift is self-evident, and it's made more endearing by her callow experimentation. Just as important as her talent, the endorphin rush of singing — a quality that unites her best work through the decades — is palpable in everything from her frantic hand gestures to the glow on her face.

Skepticism is perhaps an inevitable reaction to any artist freighted with the weight of ultimacy. The business of pop singing has long generated superlatives — Ella Fitzgerald was "the first lady of song," both Frank Sinatra and Whitney Houston were hailed as "the Voice" of their times, and Brazilian singer Milton Nascimento has been said to possess "the voice of God." Though the phrase never reached household ubiquity, the *Guinness Book of World Records* once dubbed Mariah "Songbird Supreme." These are heavy crowns. In truth, there is no such thing as a vocalist capable of everything. Voices have their boundaries, and Mariah's is no different.

Nevertheless, it was clear from the hype surrounding her self-titled debut album that she'd been groomed to be a unicorn. As if to position her as a singer first, the back of that album's cover depicts her with eyes closed, lost in song, leaning into a vintage standing microphone. The photograph conjures an association with the golden age of American pop and jazz, the microphone evoking the memory of canonical vocalists such as Sinatra and Fitzgerald. If time has challenged the hyperboles that have surrounded Mariah, it has also solidified her place within this lineage, allowing us to contemplate her alongside her most celebrated forebears as well as the nameless be-alls and end-alls not fortunate enough to live in the age of recorded sound.

Extreme talent begets extreme mythology—and as (unproven) legend would have it, Mariah hits the notes only dogs can hear, the notes that shatter glass, the notes that she says once opened a fan's garage door.[3] But of the handful of American pop singers who have been treated with this degree of reverence, few are celebrated for their artistry outside the vocal booth. Indeed, few can claim to have written all their signature songs, produced and arranged for other artists, and directed several of their own music videos, as Mariah has. Because of this paucity of precedent, it has always been easier for the casual listener to assume Mariah is an interpreter of material rather than the auteur behind it. From this vantage, her voice is a thing applied, like a veneer. It's style, not substance, a conveyor of meaning rather than its maker.

Even if we were to take Mariah's voice for granted as a mere conveyor, we'd still have to acknowledge that there's nothing effortless or unmindful about what she does with it. Singing like hers is creative and intellectual labor. In Mariah's conception, the voice is not something you're stuck with from birth but a series of guises, affectations, and masks that the artist creates. I can't think of another living pop superstar whose sound has been so propelled by the idea that a voice can be radically manipulated—that, far from being a static entity defined by the measurements enumerated in those YouTube fan videos, a voice can turn itself into something unexpected.

Listen to Mariah's discography in chronological order, and you'll find it hard not to notice the numerous vocal personas that spring up. There's the stentorian, full-throated belting of her first few albums; the fluid mix of chest and head voice deployed to masterful effect in the mid-1990s; and the delicate, foggy tones and manic cadences that predominated after the turn of the millennium. (As if this weren't chameleonic enough, the audiobook of her 2020 memoir, *The Meaning of Mariah Carey*, features her doing a hilarious impression of Grace Slick's "White Rabbit," a song that Mariah associates with her childhood.)

Knowing all her records by heart means that, at any given point, on any album, I hear the ghosts of Mariah's past as well as intimations of the ones to come. I revel in these feats of self-transformation, recognizing in them the artist's desire to leave no stone unturned, no trick untried.

Because her songwriting is so intimately connected to her singing, it too has shown an exceptional plasticity. Part of the fun of listening to Mariah is how her knowledge of genres, styles, and formats—acquired as a lonely child of divorce obsessively listening to the radio—has enabled her to craft inspired interpretations of so many kinds of songs, from slow jams to club bangers, from fiery gospel to Righteous Brothers–style tearjerkers, from girl-group pop to soft-rock power ballads, from gritty hip-hop to austere confessionals. If the voice, as the avant-garde vocalist Meredith Monk believes, is a "manifestation of the self,"[4] then the Mariah we encounter across her catalog is one of the most protean characters in modern pop—so protean that no hired hitmaker du jour could be credited with furnishing material more fitting than the singer herself could.

Here's another metaphor: when I find myself geeking out over a Mariah performance I know by heart, I like to picture her voice as a kind of cosmic seeker, stretching its tentacles into weird little pockets of sound, and her songwriting as the vessel in which its discoveries are sent back to us. At its most daring, her singing can be uncannily mimetic, bringing to bear the technique of "tone painting" found in classical music: just listen to the way her voice flutters like a butterfly on a song called "Butterfly"; how it introduces a staccato stutter to the word "unsteady" in "I Am Free"; how it lifts off into the stratosphere at the end of "Can't Let Go" to illustrate the accomplishment of impossible surrender. At its most emotional, her voice is so alive that it seems to be composing in the moment, surprising and delighting itself at every turn.

Maybe you can already tell: I've always wanted to be a singer. But I'll never call myself that. I'm trapped in a state of perpetual envy, in a body that won't make the transcendent sounds I want it to. I fling my voice in all directions, but it only goes so far. My talent isn't negligible, but neither is it exceptional, and when I'm looking for an excuse to help me accept this brutal fact, I tell myself that Mariah set the bar too high: after her, any singing worthy of the name must at least shift the molecules in the room. What business would someone like me have sounding like that anyway?

Because I've been shower-singing since childhood (and have since graduated to minor-league karaoke glory), I know the mechanics of the art well enough to intuit what it would be like for Mariah's voice to come out of my mouth. I can imagine all the cylinders that would have to be firing at once for me to phonate at that level. It's as if long-term fandom has granted me the muscle memory of a phantom sound, one I'll never produce.

Despite my modest abilities, singing has never stopped being a philosophical force in my life. In the moment when my voice meets the air, curling itself into the shape of a melody, I'm reminded I exist.

Just as I hear many Mariahs while listening to Mariah, I'm also hearing the alternate reality in which my voice can do what hers does. And nowadays, I see images of my former selves: Me looking for the just-released *Butterfly* album at a record store, if only to stare at the cover and try to persuade my dad to buy it for me. Me listening to the CD in the car as my dad, who also loves music but favors Elvis Presley, the Carpenters, and Teresa Teng, asks, "Does she have to be so *loud*?" Me sitting alone in my room mimicking the mouth-shapes of Mariah's phrasing and her signature tic: one finger pressed against her ear and another darting around busily as if to pluck notes out of the air.

One song of particular intricacy defied my lip-syncing attempts. Made amid Mariah's separation from Mottola in 1997 — a period of astonishing artistic growth — "Outside" is her account of living "somewhere halfway" between Black and white. It starts off sweet and shy, in a sotto voce that makes the words sound as if they've been covered in gauze. Her voice seems to float outside itself, unconnected to flesh. The melody, though lovely, meanders, practically hookless, like an unplanned improvisation. Then toward the end, the song suddenly finds itself, or Mariah finds herself in it. The drums crash in, and her voice bursts forth: "oh! and God knows / that you're standing on your own / blind and unguided / into a world divided you're thrown."

This climax arrives like the most deafening blast in a John Coltrane solo, turning a shriek of pain into a gorgeous sonic epiphany. It's a coming into being; where Mariah has spent the previous several minutes singing *off* her vocal cords, she's now leapt back *into* them, and they're working at full throttle. It's one of the most intense minutes on any '90s diva-pop record; in fact, despite the genre being littered with instances of decibel-spiking ostentation, I can't think of anything that quite compares. The composition itself—its languid meter, its circuitous train of thought, its abrupt shifts from serenity to turbulence, then back again—is an odd one. Though cowritten by Walter Afanasieff and coproduced by Cory Rooney, the song strikes me as far too peculiar, too *lived-in* of an achievement to have primarily originated from anywhere other than the mind of one artist. But the voice conveyed even more than the candid lyrics could. The too-muchness of the vocal was an accurate description of everything I felt but couldn't say.

When you live in a closet, you learn to look out for signs. Signs of danger. Signs of rescue. Signs of what Wayne Koestenbaum calls, in his book *The Queen's Throat*, "the pleasure gardens on the other side of trauma."[5]

Mariah's vocals seemed to be saying that the ultimate voice could also be the one that resonated on the queerest frequency. The most beloved voice could be the most freakish.

I was ten or eleven when I first heard "Outside," and I didn't realize I was responding from the outside of the song: as a Chinese American falling in love with Black American music; as a nerdy, closeted gay boy projecting his life onto a glamorous, hetero-feminine idol. It wasn't until years later that I'd find poignancy in this collision of social realities, but when I was young, I felt the connection to be intimate and private — from her heart to mine. Mariah made my outside feel like an inside. I knew if a voice were a place, I'd call hers home.

# 2

# WHAT A VOICE MEANS

In every iconic singer's career, there's a point at which she can never again claim her voice to be unrecognizable. Her sound and her name become intertwined in public consciousness — in a few elite cases, on a global scale. For all that is gained in stardom, something is lost. Day-one diehards can't help but feel a pang of longing for the time when the voice had the strangeness of the new, when it could still be possessively guarded by a coterie of obsessive listeners. And the singer has her own reasons to miss the Eden of anonymity, where she could catch an audience unawares and beguile them without having to live up to the standard her debut has enshrined.

Separating a voice from the image of its owner has been a winning premise for two TV competitions: *The Voice* and *The Masked Singer*, both of which feature contestants who perform without their faces visible. This set-up underscores the desire to experience voices on their own sonic terms, free from the racial and gendered assumptions we project onto singers' bodies, and unmediated by an industry that rushes to package creative expression for profit. There's something about a voice that asks to be heard in the purity of ignorance. I've found this to be the case in my own life as a mere karaoke hobbyist: singing in front of people who don't know I can carry a tune is endorphin-producing, no matter how nonexistent the stakes or negligible the achievement. No one expects a short, bespectacled Asian dude to sound the way I do, and I milk that surprise (that uncloseting) for all it's worth.

In his autobiography, *Hitmaker*, Tommy Mottola remembers his shock upon first hearing Mariah Carey. It wasn't just the power of her voice that startled him; it was also what he judged to be a mismatch of sound and source. The Sony Music CEO met Mariah when she accompanied Brenda K. Starr to a party. Starr—who had a hit in 1988 with the ballad "I Still Believe," and for whom Mariah sang backup—gave Mottola a copy of a demo tape containing material Mariah had written in a woodshed with a collaborator named Ben Margulies. After leaving the event, Mottola played the cassette in his limo. "The music had R&B and gospel qualities that made it seem like Brenda had given me the wrong tape," he recalls. "That couldn't be the blonde chick that I met, I thought."[1] His racial misapprehension clearly heightened the frisson, the sense of a rare and exotic discovery. He tracked Mariah down and offered her a record deal. Reflecting on this life-upending meet-cute, Mariah admitted to veteran radio DJ and TV host Donnie Simpson in 1996, "It sounds like something fabricated. It doesn't sound like a real story."[2]

Not all singers have moments of revelation that can be easily woven into their mythologies, but Mariah has several. There's the time when she was around eight years old and a friend told her, "When you sing it sounds like there are instruments with you,"[3] a poetic description that encapsulates something naïve and unschooled about how we respond to the lightning bolt of talent in our midst. There's the moment when Mariah's mother, a singer with the New York City Opera, realized that her child had a gift: while practicing a challenging aria from *Rigoletto*, Patricia Carey heard her daughter repeat a line back to her with flawless pronunciation and pitch. And in her memoir, Mariah shares an anecdote from the late '80s in which she's an audience member at a performance by the R&B star Jeffrey Osborne. While singing his hit "You Should Be Mine (The Woo Woo Song)," Osborne tosses the mic to her, and she ends up soaring into her whistle register, stunning the crowd.

As time goes by, such stories begin to function as origin myths. They're as much about talent coming into the knowledge of itself as they are about its reception by others. They also bolster the idea that certain meteoric ascents are preordained, impervious to chance. Mariah subscribed to this notion from a young age, and it's not hard to understand why. Her mother had given her a glamorous name and urged her, "Don't say '*if* I make it,' say '*when* I make it.'"[4]

The closest Mariah came to staging this illusion of out-of-the-blue emergence for a wide audience was her June 1990 performance of "America the Beautiful" at the NBA Finals — one of her first prime-time TV appearances. I use the word "illusion" because, technically, she had already arrived: her first single was released the previous month.

A eureka moment in pop, "Vision of Love" begins portentously, with a reverberating synthesizer effect that sounds like the door of a spaceship cracking open, presumably to let out the unearthly vocal specimen inside. Once the lyrics kick in, the song feels a bit too sophisticated to have been written by a teenager, but it also has the endearing quasi-maturity of a girl feverishly dreaming herself into adulthood. Young Mariah imagines romantic love as something not unlike her own impending stardom — it's "sweet destiny," a force bigger than herself. But even as that destiny dwarfs her, she describes herself as someone with agency, a kind of prophetess, responsible for manifesting "the love that came to be" through diligent prayer.

At the time of the NBA Finals, "Vision of Love" hadn't achieved mass-market saturation and Mariah wasn't yet a household name; the single was still a couple months away from topping the charts. Planted in the middle of destiny's brief (if undoubtedly agonizing) delay, this extracurricular performance was a pivotal one, undertaken with the solemnity of a maiden voyage. "America the Beautiful" might not have the prestige of "The Star-Spangled Banner," but putting her stamp on it allowed Mariah to place herself in the soul tradition of Ray Charles, whose famous 1972 version gave the song an idiosyncratic, proudly Black makeover. In his rendition, you hear an artist imprinting his sensibility — his gravelly timbre and inimitable way of lagging behind the beat — onto a standard that anyone raised in the US will have heard hundreds of times before. His approach, rooted in gospel, turns the song into a platform for individual expression and emotion, not a prompting for an easy, breezy sing-along.

Mariah was not a veteran like Charles, but her take was no less audacious. Greeted with polite applause and wearing the nondescript black bodycon dress featured on the back of her debut album, she launches confidently into her lower register, thick and imposing. As she moves through "spacious skies" and "amber waves of grain," she revises the familiar melody playfully but judiciously, her voice beginning to unfurl. "America the Beautiful" isn't known for the leaps that make the national anthem difficult for the average person to sing, so you start to doubt whether she'll manage to push the song into her upper register and bring the house down. Then it happens: she bends the song to her will. On "sea to shining sea," she turns the climactic "sea" into "sea-ahhhh . . . ," starting in her chest voice, then vaulting multiple octaves up into a whistle note of such purity it barely sounds real. The audience responds in exaltation.

Pulling off such a risky maneuver, the singer makes a bid for the listener's trust, the loyalty that will serve her well through the storms of a long career. Whistle notes—which tend to have the bright but airy ring of a kettle coming to a boil and are produced when the anterior folds of the vocal cords vibrate while the rest of the instrument stays inactive—were not entirely new to popular music. Minnie Riperton had already taken the sound to the top of the charts with 1975's "Lovin' You," and Deniece Williams had punctuated several of her songs with quick coloratura trills. But those singers had thinner timbres that exuded a sense of weightlessness and didn't tend to make use of the dark low notes and muscular belts that Mariah flaunts in her build-up of "America the Beautiful." It's the juxtaposition of these tones—her combination of the earthy with the ethereal—that makes Mariah's use of the whistle so astonishing.

There's something irrational, bizarre, and hazardous-sounding about the way Mariah hopscotches over and across vocal registers without warning or transition. You don't have to be a singer to intuit that it's a perilous act.

In the context of the climactic moment in "America the Beautiful," though, the leap is more than spectacle for its own sake. Mariah's "sea-ahhhh" evokes rolling vistas and open water. It captures the song's mix of religiosity and pride. You get the feeling that not far from Mariah's mind is the thought that maybe *she* is the majesty of which she's singing, that her sound might be vast enough to match the size of the United States. If composers such as Duke Ellington, Aaron Copland, and Charles Ives could aspire to this lofty goal with their music, is it far-fetched to claim that Mariah, in her own way, was trying to do something similar with her voice?

That rangy, belty sound *is* profoundly American—it's aggressive, attention-seeking, and vaguely imperial in a way that neatly aligns with the national persona. Thankfully, jingoistic bombast didn't turn out to be Mariah's preferred mode, and she has never again so boldly highlighted the link between her voice and the nation. Still, the idea that a voice can stand in for something greater than itself—that it can be held responsible for representing whole communities, including ones the singer may not have imagined she had anything to do with—is useful for understanding how her music has traveled across decades, demographics, and continents.

Into what sort of America had Mariah's voice arrived? As a fan with very little pop-culture memory prior to 1992 (the year I turned six), I've had to put some effort into imagining the conditions under which the earliest generation of lambs would have experienced her. In preparation for this book, I studied '80s pop and R&B by making playlists out of the top one hundred singles of each year in the decade, as if ingesting it all might help me pinpoint what was in the air—what made an artist like Mariah possible. This method of comparison only gets me so far, but it does fill in the portrait around the edges.

Mariah's vocal range alone lends her the air of a sui generis phenomenon, but influence is something she happily wears on her sleeve. She is knowingly referential, and you can hear this in the samples she uses, in the material she chooses to cover, and in the way her music is constantly in conversation with the sounds of the moment. The backdrops that frame her voice on her self-titled debut album—courtesy of dependable pop producers Narada Michael Walden (a hitmaker for Whitney Houston and Aretha Franklin) and Ric Wake (a key collaborator of Taylor Dayne)—reflect trends of the late 1980s and early '90s, marking her clearly as a product of that time. Listening to my playlists, I can hear, for instance, how the clattering percussion on her first up-tempo single, "Someday," descends directly from new jack swing, the hip-hop and R&B hybrid style pioneered by Teddy Riley, Jimmy Jam and Terry Lewis, and Babyface. She may not have been closely associated with hip-hop until later in the '90s, but already on her first release she was trying out its rhythms. On the charmingly cheesy album cut "Prisoner," you can even hear her rapping, tongue planted in cheek.

By assembling all this pre-Mariah music, I also get a panoramic view of Black women singers at the turn of the century, including the field's preponderance of underappreciated talent. Mariah's victories had the unfortunate effect of allowing her to overshadow artists who never received the resources she benefited from—some of them darker-skinned Black women who may have been held back by the industry's colorism. While vocal pyrotechnics were not a prerequisite for fame in the '80s (just as common were the easygoing, chirpy tones of Cherrelle, Patrice Rushen, and Lisa Lisa), the era did introduce a respectable number of big voices. Several of the best are little-known among young R&B lovers today: artists such as Miki Howard, a bluesy powerhouse who made several appearances on the urban chart without scoring a pop hit, and Meli'sa Morgan, an excellent singer-songwriter who faded much too quickly from the spotlight. The first few years of Mariah's fame coincided with the emergence of Lalah Hathaway, Lisa Fischer, and Rachelle Ferrell, three magnificent vocalists who have deservedly lasted as music-industry veterans but never caught on with the wider public that embraced Mariah.

Walking the ever-shifting line between symbolic Blackness and symbolic whiteness, Mariah faced the pressures of an era in which Black music's relationship with the broader American culture had reached a turning point. In his much-cited 1988 book *The Death of Rhythm and Blues*, Nelson George argues that the conglomeration of the entertainment industry, the shuttering of Black-owned mom-and-pop record stores, and the homogenization of radio playlists in the '80s (along with a host of other, less quantifiable, factors) led to a feast-or-famine mentality in the development of Black artists. This meant that while a select few Black entertainers—Michael and Janet Jackson, Prince, Lionel Richie, and Whitney Houston—were able to achieve massive popularity across demographics, creating the impression of a seismic shift in a disempowered community's fortunes, most acts lived in fear of getting dropped when they failed to immediately net a crossover hit. George's book was influential not only in its critique of corporate influences on Black music but also in its conviction that something valuable and authentic had been lost in post-soul R&B.

What was Black music if its most visible progenitors were a self-proclaimed "king of pop" rumored to have bleached his own skin (Michael Jackson); an adult-contemporary diva who was booed at the Soul Train Awards by members of her own community, some of whom called her "Whitey" (Whitney Houston); and an Englishman who, a year before Mariah's debut, became the first white guy to win the American Music Award for Favorite Soul/R&B Male Artist (George Michael)? For some, Mariah was just another major-label cash cow watering down Black music and hastening its decline.

Ironically, in Mottola's view, it was the record label — more than Black music or the barely adult Mariah herself — that was the vulnerable party. For years, Columbia Records, the Sony Music subsidiary to which Mariah was signed, had been coasting on the sales of mostly white male legacy acts, such as Billy Joel, Bob Dylan, and Bruce Springsteen. The company was losing out to its main competitor, Warner Bros., in the battle for new talent. And despite having been involved with the likes of Billie Holiday, Mahalia Jackson, and Aretha Franklin several decades earlier, the label had a reputation for making poor decisions when it came to these women's artistry. It was Columbia that had refused to record Holiday's controversial anti-lynching song "Strange Fruit," and that saddled Franklin with a stuffy supper-club repertoire. The company also had no significant track record with contemporary Black female musicians.

Mottola's professional insecurity compounded these pressures. Lacking the usual MBA pedigree, he had been an out-of-the-box choice to replace previous Sony CEO Walter Yetnikoff, an erratic, sometimes abusive figure. Mottola came in surrounded by naysayers who balked at his attempts to transform an office culture bogged down by what he considered a complacent, aging staff. His antidote to stagnation was not creative risk. Early in his tenure, Mottola saw how an artist's popularity could be derailed by an unexpected fit of eccentricity. His autobiography bemoans the left turns taken by George Michael and R&B singer-songwriter Terence Trent D'Arby, both of whom rebelled against the star-making machinery.

From the outset, Mottola intended to make Mariah "bigger than Whitney,"[5] and that meant every step of her journey through public life had to be choreographed with market domination as a guiding principle. Sony executives nicknamed her "the Franchise."[6] In Mottola's book, he remembers telling her: "You can have it *all*. All markets. All demographics. You can have it all like no other artist who's ever come before you."[7] Such maniacal ambition, normalized in a business run by profit-driven moguls, presumes common-denominator palatability to be a self-evident virtue.

Mariah's own attitudes, both then and now, are understandably conflicted. She bristled at the company's thinly veiled requests for a whiter direction and insists that her tastes were always aligned with the Black styles she was discouraged from wholeheartedly pursuing. But in a crucial sense, her high hopes for herself dovetailed with Mottola's. In the late '80s, she was invited to audition for Def Jam, the iconic hip-hop label that broke Run-D.M.C. into the mainstream. Despite the financial challenges she faced as a teenager doing odd jobs and background-vocal gigs in Manhattan, Mariah turned down that opportunity.[8]

Her idea of success was fully formed, and Sony was ready to make those dreams come true. According to a 1991 *New York Times* article, Sony's marketing campaign for Mariah was "rumored to be one of the most expensive for a new artist."[9] And in a scandal-stoking feature in *Vanity Fair* from 1996, Mottola is portrayed as a showbiz mafioso who authorized "the expenditure of $800,000 to produce her debut album, $500,000 to redo the video for her first single, and an additional $1 million in promotion and marketing to grease the launch of both."[10]

What would Mariah's early music have sounded like if she'd started out at a smaller label with lower financial stakes, a commitment to Black music, and a youthful roster? We can only wonder. Mariah set her sights on the highest rung of the ladder. As someone who'd gained much of her musical knowledge by fanatically listening to the radio, she had good reason to believe in the power and glory of hit records that saturate cultural consciousness. These records had thrown her a lifeline during a tumultuous, peripatetic childhood marred by racism, economic instability, and domestic turmoil. Her fixation on hits would inform her artistry as much as it would enable her commercial triumphs.

Once a voice slots itself into a particular historical context, a network of associations closes in around it. From then on, it becomes hard to hear the voice again as pure sound; cultural and aesthetic labels are assigned to it, generating meanings that travel beyond the singer's intentions.

As soon as Mariah hit the scene, she was largely perceived as a ballad singer — a pigeonhole that, in the estimation of skeptics, shrunk her to the size of a Hallmark card. Singing with old-fashioned earnestness about loves lost, found, and unwisely prolonged, she became easy to dismiss as juvenile and saccharine. While Mariah did score a few up-tempo hits at the start of her career, ballads constitute the heart of her early discography, and their omnipresence makes it all but impossible to love her if you can't get in touch with the sappiest parts of yourself.

The most starkly beautiful of these ballads is "Vanishing," which originated from the fateful demo tape that secured her Columbia deal. Part of what's striking about "Vanishing" is its restraint: not only is it one of the few Mariah songs to feature a stripped-down arrangement of vocals and piano, but it also spends half of its length — two verses draped across two languid minutes — withholding the customary thrills of belting, whistling, and ornate riffing. Those things come in time, but first Mariah narrates a tale of ghostly dimensions with slow, capacious lines that summon the memory of a faded love.

When a singer like Mariah decides to bring a boil down to a simmer, you can't help but take notice. The first half of "Vanishing" is worth considering as Mariah's take on the Great American Songbook, a concerted display of classic pop composition sturdy enough to fit any talented singer's voice. It starts as a grim torch song that you could imagine coming out of the mouth of Frank Sinatra or Nancy Wilson. Like some of the gloomiest jazz standards — say, "Angel Eyes" or "The Night We Called It a Day" — "Vanishing" conveys romantic loss through metaphors of physical disappearance and occluded perception. Mariah strains to "hear the distant laughter" of her lover, whom she describes as "suddenly hard to see."

The austere piano arrangement, played by respected studio musician Richard Tee, gives us space to hang on every one of Mariah's breaths and syllables. You can sense how much she has labored over the writing of these words in the very deliberate way she pronounces them: the affricates in "recapture" and "enraptured" are delivered with a theatrical emphasis, while "faster," uttered in both the second and final verse, breaks up the steady pace by taking on serpentine melismatic shapes. Even more effective is the way Mariah gives us a feeling of irresolution in her line endings. The first sentence concludes with "would" ("If I could recapture all of the memories / and bring them to life surely I *would*"), but the word is suspended in air, without a conventional end-rhyme, until "misunderstood" comes halfway through the second verse fifty seconds later. Then, charging into the bridge, Mariah unleashes her first belted high notes on "you're," a full-throated cry that fractures the song so dramatically that she doesn't even bother to complete the thought.

"Vanishing" shows Mariah was capable at a young age of an elegantly crafted lyric. But this wasn't the norm for her in those days, nor did it have to be. In another extraordinary ballad from this period, the 1991 single "Can't Let Go," the lyrics are merely serviceable, riddled with clichés and even some recycled language ("capture," a key word in "Vanishing," is prominent here too, this time in the chorus). But amid everything that's going on in this lushly produced track, such straightforwardness is a virtue. How banal it is, ultimately, to experience the humiliation of being hung up on someone who, in Mariah's words, doesn't "even know I'm alive."

If "Vanishing" is about the fitful process of a lover's disappearance, "Can't Let Go" is about how the one who's been left behind turns the void into something graspable. Instead of assuming spectral form, the ex in "Can't Let Go" is hauntingly present. "Every night I see you in my dreams," Mariah coos; "there you are," she sighs.

Heartache may be the subject here, but there's a reason the song's paradoxically lulling qualities make so much emotional sense: wallowing is just a perverse form of self-soothing. Like the other love songs on Mariah's ballad-laden second album, *Emotions* (many coproduced by Walter Afanasieff, one of the singer's most important creative partners during the early '90s), "Can't Let Go" begins by establishing an environment: echoing synthesizers that conjure a windswept landscape; a gently plucked guitar and a few whistle notes buried deep down in the mix, creating a sensation of space and distance.

Almost a full minute goes by before the percussion drops in, turning this languorous mood piece into a sprint, the beat subdivided minutely by clicks and chimes. Where "Vanishing" was punctuated with heavy silences, "Can't Let Go" is all forward motion, thanks in part to its contemporary R&B style; in fact, it's a revision of Keith Sweat's sensual 1987 hit "Make It Last Forever," with the seduction replaced by a heaping dose of sorrow.

Much of the brilliance lies in the web of studio effects that shrouds Mariah's raw lead vocal. This is clear in the way she and Afanasieff handle the track's conclusion, which revolves around a whistle note so piercingly high it transmits both agony and ecstasy. The sting of pain is swathed in thickly arranged harmonies, then encircled by that unrelenting drum-machine pattern, which responds to the singer's lament with an assurance that time will keep marching on, regardless of whether she wants it to. These details make the song devastatingly good, and they reveal Mariah's instincts as a recording artist, one who knows how to get voice, song, and sonic detail to snap into place.

*Emotions* earned Mariah a Grammy nomination for Producer of the Year (Non-Classical), making her one of the first women and one of the youngest artists to compete in that category. This continues to be an unsung milestone in her career: female pop and R&B stars were not known for taking on such an authoritative role in the studio, the '80s artists Teena Marie and Angela Winbush being two notable exceptions. If you ask me, "Can't Let Go" should have secured Mariah a win. It shows that she has always been, as much as anything else, a studio magician.

Within the confines of what we call "the ballad," Mariah found abundance. Listen to "Vision of Love," "Vanishing," and "Can't Let Go" side by side, and you'll hear three different approaches to this song category so frequently treated like a monolith. And even if we were to limit ourselves to the first three of Mariah's fifteen studio albums, there are even more varieties: the soul throwback "If It's Over," cowritten with Carole King; the funereal jazz elegy "The Wind," sung over a melody from the '50s by pianist and Chet Baker sideman Russell Freeman; and the gospel tour de force "Anytime You Need a Friend," which ends with an explosive, riff-filled climax that brought Mariah as close as she'd ever been to the music of the Black church.

Eventually, as frequent Mariah collaborator Jermaine Dupri has said, she got "tired of being called 'the ballad queen.'"[11] Nevertheless, few contemporary pop stars have explored as many facets of the ballad as she has with as much zeal.

How does an artist grow weary of something she has mastered? Mariah has never abandoned ballads, but her impatience at being so strongly associated with them might seem out of character for an artist whose work is a testament to the inexhaustibility of the form. There are many reasons why singers like Mariah gravitate to ballads. There's a luxury in not having to compete with a loud, hectic beat, and the spacious lines and opportunity to sustain long, legato notes encourage listeners to pay close attention to vocal nuances that often go unnoticed in up-tempo songs. In all their various incarnations, ballads have allowed Mariah to sing in the ways she uniquely can. And yet the mandate to churn them out on album after album — to produce gigantic emotions on demand — has at times exhausted and irritated her.

Part of her resistance must have to do with the fact that Mottola zeroed in on a certain kind of ballad as the ideal vehicle for Mariah's voice, and sometimes asked her to write them at the drop of a hat. Of the twelve charting singles from her first three studio albums, eight are slow-burning paeans to passion, heartbreak, and old-fashioned survival. All eight fit comfortably in the realm of adult contemporary, a radio format that was known for catering to white women between the ages of twenty-five and forty-nine. Mariah's demo tape was full of ballads, but what may have begun for her as a way of proving herself was for Mottola a branding strategy. After her debut album had already been sent to be mastered and manufactured, he ordered Mariah to go back into the studio to quickly cut one more monster ballad, hoping to make the fairly unorthodox move of introducing her to the world with two of them in a row.[12] The result was her second chart-topper, "Love Takes Time," a tearjerker that manages to feel dashed-off and expertly polished all at once.

The long evolution of ballads in American music has touched nearly every popular genre. By the time Mariah became associated with the form, the typical ballad had acquired an operatic intensity that in previous decades — when Frank Sinatra's molasses-slow saloon songs or Elvis Presley's sweetly pining "Love Me Tender" were the prototypes — would probably have sounded too unhinged for the airwaves. As scholar David Metzer has noted in his studies on balladry, the word "power" was attached as a prefix in the '70s, codifying an ultra-melodramatic variant that first gained popularity with adult-contemporary singers such as Barry Manilow, then made its way into arena rock. (That latter development was met with homophobia in high places: no less a rock-and-roll institution than critic Lester Bangs weighed in on the rise of the power ballad by declaring that "faggots love it.")[13] These songs are calibrated for maximum ache, but they're also all about triumph, the swelling strings, wailing guitars, and flamboyant vocals often drowning out the vulnerability of the lyrics. Mariah's small repertoire of covers includes several relatively faithful, lovely renditions of male rock ballads she would have heard as a kid — Badfinger's "Without You," Journey's "Open Arms," Def Leppard's "Bringing on the Heartbreak," Foreigner's "I Want to Know What Love Is." Her song selections indicate that she was conscious, on some level, not only of the balladic lineage that preceded her, but also of under-acknowledged continuities between rock and R&B, and between masculine and feminine expressions of longing.

Most of Mariah's ballads are indeed focused on the purging of private emotions. But there are also quite a few written with a second-person address aimed at the masses, songs possessed of what could be called "all-purpose feeling." I must admit that the further Mariah gets from expressing her inner life, and the more "universal" she tries to be, the quicker I tend to lose interest, and "Hero" — the biggest single off her third studio album, *Music Box*, and perhaps the most internationally well-known of all her ballads — is the point at which my fandom gets tested and strained. I'm not alone in my lack of enthusiasm for its prettily banal melody and platitudinal lyrics: in her memoir, Mariah says that she felt the song was "schmaltzy"[14] after writing it, while Mottola remembers her dismissing it as "too white-bread"[15] and supposes that "she might've been embarrassed by it in front of the hip-hop community."

"Hero" is one of the few Mariah songs that lends itself to being sung by other divas. In fact, it's been performed live, on separate occasions, by no less a trinity than Aretha Franklin, Gladys Knight, and Patti LaBelle. Part of what makes the song so adaptable is the fact that it wasn't meant to be Mariah's hit in the first place. Mottola had asked her and Afanasieff to compose a title theme for the 1992 movie *Hero*, starring Dustin Hoffman and Geena Davis, to be recorded by Gloria Estefan. On hearing the results, Mottola felt it was too much of a classic for his wife not to keep.

One gets the sense that what Mottola was responding to

was how applicable "Hero" is to any listener's struggle. Devoid of references to economic degradation or social injustice, it could just as easily be speaking about the alienation of upper-middle-class suburbanites as about a hardscrabble existence in a disenfranchised community. And though it may be unfair to deride it for its probably unintentional political connotations, its message—that individuals should find the means within themselves to per-severe—echoes ideas about personal accountability that helped dismantle the social safety net in the 1980s and '90s.

It's easy to resent how "Hero" smooths away Mariah's edges and suppresses her quirks, feeding into false conceptions of her as a bland, culturally neutral everywoman. But that's not the whole story. While there are certain lambs who think Mariah's later R&B and hip-hop work represents a truer version of her artistry than her adult-contemporary ballads, it is "Hero" that many fans—both hard-core and casual, in the US and abroad—cite when they say the singer has gotten them through hard times. For Mariah, who has long bemoaned the deficit of control she experienced during this phase of her career, it's yet another lesson that the control she sought is illusory in at least one fundamental sense. The real-world impact of a pop song often has little to do with the artist's original intentions for it or estimations of it.

For better or worse, "Hero" became the quintessential Mariah ballad during these early years. Since its release, she has been invited several times to perform it in response to momentous junctures in social and pop-cultural history: at the 9/11 benefit *America: A Tribute to Heroes*, at Barack Obama's inauguration, at Michael Jordan's final NBA All-Star game, at a fundraising event during the COVID-19 pandemic. You might say that the song has served a pub-lic function not unlike that of a patriotic anthem: it's a morale booster for a country run on compulsory optimism and a culture that often prioritizes self-actualization over community building. Its success solidified an impression of Mariah's voice as a kind of shield, an object of titanium strength. In the coming years, as she began to let her guard down, the falseness of this impression gave her fuel: it became something to work against, to disprove. There were other ways her voice could sound, other things it could signify, and it wasn't long before those possibilities revealed themselves.

# 3

# OTHER SOUNDS, OTHER REALMS

It's hard to love pop music without loving its formulas. The elements that make most mainstream hits recognizable as such are still inescapable, even as new trends take hold, and even as certain visionaries push the art form into less predictable territory. These elements allow us to feel at home in the music, regardless of whether we're familiar with what's on the charts in any given week.

There is, for instance, the matter of time. Most pop singles still fall somewhere within the range of three to five minutes, a convention that traces its origins back to outmoded technologies (the capacity of 78 and 45 rpm records imposed limits on song length) and commercial considerations (radio programmers are disinclined to linger too long on anything, fearing that the listener will get bored and turn the dial).[1] This concision may have been born of industrial imperatives that have little to do with art, but its effects are undeniably aesthetic. Songs that are easy to digest are also easy to remember, and the tenacity with which a tune can lodge itself in our neural pathways helps lock in its enduring pleasures. The classic ABABCB structure, built on a relay of verse, chorus, and bridge, further facilitates memorization. The fact that pop songs can be fully possessed by the mind gives them a talismanic power. And the way they spiral around repeated melodies and phrases can make us feel as if they're playing on a loop, an impression of endlessness that belies their brevity.

Inseparable from these parameters is what they're tasked with containing: emotion, the lifeblood of pop. The music's rigid package can give our inchoate feelings shape and definition, a beginning and an ending. Falling under the spell of an effective pop song can be like getting a momentary handle on some thorny issue that years of therapy and prayer have failed to solve.

Mariah Carey knows how to work the constraints of the pop song to her advantage. Sometimes she'll push against them, but she's also perfectly happy to color within the lines. At her best, she seems plugged into a platonic ideal of the pop song floating somewhere out in the ether. Despite its stylistic variety, her body of work hangs together by virtue of her preternatural proficiency with the laws governing what sounds *good* and what's *catchy*, culturally circumscribed standards that nevertheless exert a gravitational pull whenever we hear something that fits the description. This phenomenon helps explain Mariah's tendency, both in concert and on social media, to treat her fans to a cappella snippets of songs she doesn't intend to perform in full. Teasing these excerpts wouldn't be much fun if the tunes weren't so airtight and the lines so sticky, if the decontextualized fragments didn't maintain their allure even when tossed out like party favors.

Like most pop perfectionists, Mariah is an expert at making songs that are closed systems. Her choices sound both deliberate and inevitable. Each moment has its own logic and charisma, and even the ad-libs—the "doo-doo-doo-dums" and "ah-ahs"—are designed for virality. There's something companionable about this, and something incredibly intrusive too. As scholar Gary Burns has noted, the word "hook" — that descriptor for passages in pop music that stick in our brains — "connotes being caught or trapped, as when a fish is hooked, and also addiction, as when one is hooked on a drug."[2]

Music that generates this type of dependency is not readily associated with creative risk. Pop musicians are often criticized for being formulaic and manipulative, for taking advantage of the listener's craving for familiarity. But just a few years into her career, Mariah would indicate she also had an appetite for experimentation. If her best-known material reveals her attentiveness to the radio, her dance remixes signal her indebtedness to the club — a Dionysian domain of entertainment culture less encumbered by sales stats or traditional song form, a place where the musical id could be set loose. This same freedom is shared by the traditions of a much less secular space: the church, which would serve as inspiration for some of Mariah's most uninhibited singing. These seemingly antithetical but in fact interrelated milieus were frontiers where she could explore her artistry beyond the strictures of the hit factory.

Growing up, I was only faintly aware that Mariah's remixes existed. When my family got internet access in the mid-1990s, listservs and chat groups were emerging as oases of community in the strange new digital wilderness. These forums drew lambs from every corner of the world, and some of the most fanatical were given to dissecting the contents of Mariah's maxi-singles, remix-packed releases that I couldn't find in my youth, which was spent mostly in the suburban American South and Kuala Lumpur,

Malaysia. It wasn't until my early adulthood, when a lot of rare music became available through torrents and You-Tube uploads, that I got a chance to listen to these recordings that had seemed so mythical to me. It was then that I realized the extent to which Mariah had reenvisioned so many of her signature hits, sometimes giving them two or three extreme makeovers on a single disc.

With *Music Box*, Mariah began to exert an unusual amount of control over her remixes—an irony, considering the album is one of her least adventurous and is perhaps still best known for that white-elephant ballad "Hero." She unveiled her unorthodox approach with one of the few tracks on the album that counts as an artistic breakthrough. Released as *Music Box*'s lead single in the summer of 1993, "Dreamlover" was Mariah's first collaboration with Dave "Jam" Hall, a producer who had perfected a mix of gritty beats and sweet R&B melodies loosely known as "hip-hop soul." This was the first time she had teamed up with a hitmaker who operated primarily in the realms of rap and R&B.

"Dreamlover" has a stronger vintage flavor than Hall's tracks for Mary J. Blige and Father MC, two Uptown Records stars who caught Mariah's attention in the early '90s. The song derives its throwback appeal from a looped sample of "Blind Alley," a 1971 soul classic by the Emotions that has been frequently referenced by rap artists. Much of the charm of "Dreamlover" lies in the ease it projects, despite the fact that the lyrics are preoccupied not with the fulfillment of romance but with an unsatiated longing for it ("I need you so desperately," goes the chorus). The music video—which marked Mariah's first time working with director Diane Martel, who would later be instrumental in refashioning Mariah's image for hip-hop audiences — shows the singer prancing in a field of grass and flowers in a long-sleeve shirt tied above her midriff. The girl-next-door imagery matches the sound: apart from a few sky-scraping notes, "Dreamlover" is more girl-group confection than tour de force, with a main melody that falls within a reasonably comfortable range and a chorus delivered with gently sun-kissed background vocals.

David Morales's Def Club Mix of "Dreamlover" is an altogether different experience. Nearly eleven minutes long, the remix and its four-on-the-floor thump call forth images of sweaty, murkily lit nightlife, a world far removed from the open-air setting of the "Dreamlover" video. The first few minutes foreground Morales, who attacks the listener with an antic collage of blips and bleeps. A Brooklyn-born Puerto Rican American DJ, Morales had immersed himself in New York City's club scene in the '8os. While frequenting legendary spots such as the Loft and Paradise Garage, he became acquainted with house music pioneer Frankie Knuckles, who was keeping the urban dance scene exciting in the wake of disco's demise. Soon, Morales was a celebrated figure in his own right. The delirium of his take on "Dreamlover" established him as someone who could bring out a hint of the surreal in Mariah.

House music has long had access to powerful voices, but the singers largely remained in the shadows, subordinated to the DJ's or the producer's clanging beats. Because the music was not centered on stars or their images, and instead emphasized fluidity between bodies of work, vocalists (many of them Black women) often did not receive recognition commensurate with their contributions. The plus-sized singer Martha Wash, for example, was notoriously represented by a svelte model in the video for C+C Music Factory's crossover hit "Gonna Make You Sweat (Everybody Dance Now)," rendering her an apparition in her own showcase.

With someone like Mariah on the mic, anonymity isn't really an option. She stretches her voice across Morales's track with a lusty eagerness, turning the sweet romanticism of "Dreamlover" into something feral. Adjusting the melody and her intonation, she reimagines herself as a femme fatale. On the retooled chorus, pitched lower than the original, her husky tones are reminiscent of Lauren Bacall—not a far-fetched association, given Mariah's childhood love of classic Hollywood stars. And during the breakdown, when much of the instrumentation drops out, Mariah is all but panting as she commands the lover to "come and take me, take me, take me . . . baby won't you take me away!" If the album version of "Dreamlover" poses its "you" as the figment of a schoolgirl's imagination, the Def Club Mix makes the beloved's presence palpable through sheer force of desire.

In an era when house remixes were important promotional tools for pop artists hoping to make inroads into the gay club scene, Mariah forged a chemistry with Morales as strong as any she would share with future collaborators. "Dreamlover" gives us a glimpse at the heights they would scale together. Over the next few years, they'd create the house version of 1995's "Always Be My Baby," a trippy space odyssey whose melody bears only a passing resemblance to that of the hit song, and a 2000 remix of "Can't Take That Away (Mariah's Theme)" that turns one of Mariah's most self-pitying survival anthems into a series of thunderous, gospel-powered climaxes.

As someone who came into pop consciousness in the '80s, Mariah grew up at a time when remixes were becoming a mainstream phenomenon. Nile Rodgers's version of Duran Duran's "The Reflex" was all over the radio, and Jimmy Jam and Terry Lewis reimagined George Michael's "Monkey" so elaborately that they raised the bar for creativity in the remix field. But Mariah went further than her peers, treating remixes not as an occasional indulgence but as a centerpiece of her art. To understand her stature as a remix queen, you must know how unusual it was for one of the busiest pop stars in the world to rewrite melodies and record new vocals for so many of her songs. Mariah handles her remixes as a great interpreter might approach a cover of someone else's composition. She flips her own music in the same way Aretha Franklin reinvented Otis Redding's "Respect" and Simon & Garfunkel's "Bridge Over Troubled Water," with an ear for surprise and possibility. In an interview, Morales said of their work together: "That was the first time that a singer came into the studio to re-sing a record. That changed the whole idea of what remixing was . . . Nobody heard Mariah Carey sing like that."[3]

This strategy wasn't common, but it wasn't without precedent. Remixing has its roots in Jamaican music culture of the 1940s and '50s, when DJs would cobble together multiple songs and excise their less-danceable sections to create a seamless experience for clubbers. This art form had to be witnessed live. But when that art migrated to the US and became prominent during the disco era, the word "remix," once a little-known music industry term, came to take on different meanings — an evolution captured on wax. DJ Walter Gibbons broke ground by twisting Loleatta Holloway's "Hit and Run" into unrecognizable shape, abandoning much of the original melody and centering the track on sighs and exclamations, with little regard for lyrical coherence. This recording and others like it drew attention to the ecstatic properties of the twelve-inch remix, an extended format that served as an ideal soundtrack to those sex- and drug-fueled trance states that can make time melt away on the dance floor.

House music may have represented the margins for a singer of Mariah's eminence, but to its fans, it was the center of the universe — and Mariah gave it the reverence it deserved. Music critic Craig Seymour, one of the most eloquent champions of her remixes, told me:

> Black gay men were the first to appreciate all that she was bringing to the table, because these remixes were playing in the spaces where we congregated. We knew all the references. It was that familiar voice we heard on the radio, but suddenly it was speaking to us in our world. It was an incredible moment of Black gay aesthetics being mainstreamed while at the same time being obscured, because none of the critics at the time were able to make these connections.[4]

But what had started as an insular subculture also had the potential to be an all-embracing experience: house held within it the promise of music at its most inclusive. As scholar Tim Lawrence recalls of the New York dance scene in the early '90s, "It seemed as though house music contained everything anyone could want from music . . . It sounded as if the whole world, the whole of a cosmopolitan community, was contained within that music."[5]

Even fans with no apparent stake in the queer politics of

house can find something interesting in Mariah's remixes. In the contrasts between a song's original and alternate versions, you hear how the closed system of pop music can be pried open. Every moment that through endless repetition has come to sound like a foregone conclusion is in fact a choice among an array of options. Yet even as Mariah saw the remix as an avenue of creative freedom, the format would have marked her as frivolous in the eyes of the white male critical establishment—if they had cared to listen. Rock was still the go-to genre among most critics in the '90s, and the album was the privileged object. Anti-disco sentiment, which had emerged out of a brew of homophobia and racism at the end of the '70s, was alive and well more than a decade later, resulting in a dearth of serious criticism and journalism on dance music.

It takes an artist who can authoritatively occupy multiple styles to show us just how straitjacketing musical categories can be. My favorite among Mariah's early remixes does that. It comes courtesy of David Cole and Robert Clivillés, dance-music superstars whose impact on Mariah was as large as Morales's. The C+C club version of "Anytime You Need a Friend" (another song that originated on *Music Box*) is wall-to-wall Mariah: there's barely an inch of the track that isn't covered in her riffing and caterwauling. If her collaborations with Morales are built on a give-and-take between producer and vocalist, with Mariah disappearing for stretches at a time to cede ground to the maestro's noodling, this remix suggests the forbearance of collaborators who knew that all they had to do was give the singer a big canvas.

Cole and Clivillés, the men behind C+C Music Factory's "Gonna Make You Sweat," had been responsible for most of the significant club-oriented tracks on Mariah's first three albums, including "Emotions" and "Make It Happen." Their musicianship (particularly that of Cole) is most evident in this take on "Anytime You Need a Friend." Cole, a Black gay man from Tennessee who honed his craft as a church keyboardist in the '80s, opens with a build-up consisting of only piano and vocals, giving Mariah a long runway from which to blast off, before a swirling beat changes the course of the track a minute in.

Kicking a song off with vocal fireworks is a strategy that Cole and Clivillés had employed three years earlier in their remix of "Emotions," which features a sparsely accompanied opening section (later memorably sampled in Drake's 2018 song "Emotionless") in which Mariah plunges from the top of her belting register down to the basement of her range. This gutsy intro recalls the work of disco queens she admired, such as Jocelyn Brown, whose hit "Somebody Else's Guy" was an inspiration for these wailing preludes. But this is just a taste of what's to come. The remix of "Anytime You Need a Friend" doesn't follow the classic arc of a Mariah vocal, which tends to build at a systematic pace, saving its money notes for the grand finale. This performance charts its own anarchic path—a controlled collision of climaxes. In the final passage, at which point we're almost worn out by Mariah's athletic exertions, the diva decides she wants to time travel to the golden age of jazz. For two minutes, she scats with enough confidence (drawn from the years she spent improvising with her mother's jazz musician friends as a teenager) to approximate Ella Fitzgerald and Sarah Vaughan.

A mosaic of African American music, the "Anytime You Need a Friend" club mix demonstrates the interconnectedness of gospel, R&B, house, and jazz with an ease that could come only from a singer who loves all these traditions — and understands that what unites them is their rootedness in improvisation and their responsiveness to the energies of a crowd. It doesn't seem to matter to Mariah that these styles are emblematic of divergent worldviews, gospel being a conduit to the divine and house being a purveyor of earthly pleasures.

The physical endurance she maintains over the course of this eleven-minute track lends weight to the song's idealistic pronouncements on friendship. You *feel* the commitment it takes to love someone through hard times. The metaphor of Mariah's vocal labors can be extended to the clubbers whose bodies the song aims to activate. As journalist Barry Laine noted in his coverage of the disco era, "The body reaches a point when it goes beyond exhaustion, exceeds its boundaries, and rather than tiring, works harder and produces more."[6] In the same way that Mariah pushes her voice to the brink, the track throws us into a state of ecstatic fatigue.

I didn't grow up enjoying disco or house, and I suspect that the apathy I felt toward these genres early in my life was partially the result of the same internalized homophobia that made me wary of Mariah's most sentimental ballads, the homophobia that has long kept dance music on the margins of respectability. But what I've come to love in these remixes is the feeling that I'm rummaging in a drawer full of her drafts, notes, and false starts. In C+C's "Anytime You Need a Friend," you get the sense that she's not interested in creating a smooth, cohesive experience so much as flooding your ears with every idea she couldn't cram into the album version. Most of Mariah's best music is characterized by precision, but these tracks are so loose and reckless—with minutes' worth of vamping that feel defiantly unnecessary—it's as if you're watching a great artist splatter paint on a wall.

House's electronic elements have sometimes been derided as mechanistic and inhuman, but there's a live-wire immediacy in these recordings. In them, you get to hear Mariah navigate mazelike soundscapes with a moment-to-moment, pulse-by-pulse alertness. You start to wonder: How many different places can she take this melody? How will she keep this going? Listening to her on this track, I'm overwhelmed by the thought that her voice—and, by extension, music itself—are vital energies without limit or end.

This indefatigable keeping things going is evident in more than the remixes. Mariah cultivated the virtue of stamina on a broader scale, as one of her defining character traits. Halfway into the '90s, she had laid claim to the decade, having cranked out one album a year from 1990 to 1995, and having taken nine singles to the top of the pop charts within that same period. I'm not sure how much chart success alone can guarantee an artist a permanent place in pop-historical memory (my music-loving nineteen-year-old cousin grew up in a much more culturally segmented time, and when I last spoke to him, he couldn't name more than a few of Mariah's hits), but the fact that Mariah spent 467 weeks on the *Billboard* Hot 100 in the '90s alone— that's almost as many weeks as there are in a decade— does give some sense of the unstoppable engine she was believed to be, and of the fuel needed to ensure that engine could be relied on to keep running.

Number 1 hits aren't easy to achieve, no matter how much they may benefit from corporate prioritization or string-pulling. Nor does the labor end in the recording booth. Each new high gives rise to another season of publicity, another round of live performances that can wear out the singer's voice, and another level of public scrutiny — not to mention the risk of oversaturation. While the masses may have felt inundated with her sound and image, Mariah herself has said that, in her captivity, she wasn't even cognizant of how famous she'd become. In her memoir, she recounts heading to Schenectady, New York, to record a Thanksgiving special that aired a few months after the release of *Music Box*. She was shocked by the crowds on the streets and the barricades erected to protect her from them. "I had no comprehension of the impact my music and I were making on the outside world," she writes. "Did Tommy know I would be easier to control if I were kept ignorant of the full scope of my power?"[7]

Mariah's inner life was a mystery. In 1993, she married Tommy Mottola in a ceremony modeled on the wedding of Princess Diana and Prince Charles. The fifty-one-acre estate the couple purchased in Bedford, New York, had become Mariah's prison; she would later refer to it as "Sing Sing," since she often locked herself in the studio there, partly to satisfy the unabating demand for new material, but also to escape her marital troubles. It's eerie to listen to the exuberance of the remixes and know that their joyous sound emanated from the mind of an unhappy young woman who wasn't even allowed to enjoy a night out with her friends. Doubters may find this sad irony to be evidence of insincerity or fakeness in Mariah's music. For me, the fact that Mariah sounds so elated on these records points to her brilliance as a pop illusionist — and to music's power to meet emptiness with plenitude, to enact the kinds of liberation often denied its makers.

We're talking about transcendence here, so it's natural we'd end up discussing spirituality. God takes center stage in the follow-up to *Music Box*: 1994's mega-selling *Merry Christmas*. Mariah was hesitant to make a holiday record. She thought it would be unusual for an artist with only three studio albums to release Christmas music, typically the terrain of legacy artists running low on fresh material. But Mottola insisted, and the result is yet another example of Mariah seizing upon what some might consider a minor, secondary project as an opportunity to break away from the adult-contemporary formulas that had come to define her.

The three new songs that Mariah and Walter Afanasieff wrote for the album are conspicuously varied in approach: there's the nostalgia-infused, Phil Spector–inspired "All I Want for Christmas Is You," now the most famous of all Mariah songs; the yearning ballad "Miss You Most (At Christmas Time)"; and the choral hymn "Jesus Born on This Day," which has a general stateliness that would fit on the setlist of most mainline church services. Only a handful of cuts explicitly reference the sound of the African American church. But the influence is pronounced enough to remind listeners that Mariah is a devoted student of the music.

Modern dance music has long been entwined with gospel, and in a few instances a gospel song has shot to the top of the dance charts (as with the case of Sounds of Blackness's "The Pressure Pt. 1," from 1991). Fittingly, Mariah's forays into Christian music served a similar function as her club remixes: they gave her a measure of freedom she didn't find in pop radio. It was David Cole who initially brought out a Pentecostal fervor in Mariah's voice: you hear it in the growled bridge of "Make It Happen," and throughout that epic "Anytime You Need a Friend" remix. Here, the most straight-ahead gospel moment is a version of the seldom-recorded African American spiritual "Jesus Oh What a Wonderful Child," an out-of-the-box selection for a pop star's holiday album. If Mariah's hits have the expensive glossiness of a multiplex movie, this song aims for something a little bit closer to documentary verisimilitude; it's special for having been recorded not in a studio, like the rest of *Merry Christmas*, but in a church. Backed up by the glorious gospel-trained singers Kelly Price, Shanrae Price, and Melonie Daniels, Mariah is intent on proving just how convincingly she can catch the holy spirit.

The outro, performed over the kind of hectic, dou-ble-time vamp common in gospel music, demonstrates that she could move beyond imitation toward unselfconscious embodiment. As innocent as all this may sound, there's a degree of danger in the song that's both creative and per-sonal — a risk of appropriation. Mariah did not grow up in a Black church; she was raised primarily by her Irish Cath-olic mother. Though her Nana Reese, a great-aunt on her father's side, had been a pastor in Harlem, it wasn't until the early 2000s that Mariah recommitted to her faith and started attending services at True Worship Church World-wide Ministries in East New York. From the beginning of her career, though, she professed her admiration for gos-pel legends the Clark Sisters and Vanessa Bell Armstrong, both of whom were immersed in the innovative musical styles of the Church of God in Christ (COGIC). She made a point of surrounding herself with and learning from bona fide church talent such as Kelly Price, who had also been raised COGIC and had undergone some training by Clark Sisters matriarch Mattie Moss Clark in her early years.

Mariah's buoyant, bell-like tones contrast with the sound of prototypical COGIC singers. Known for its use of raspy hollers, whoops, and squalls, the COGIC performance style is built around spectacles of spiritual catharsis that are sustained with a theatrical, sometimes implicitly carnal tension. While Mariah could power-belt with the best of them, her tone is unfailingly smooth and pretty (to the point of sounding a little vain), no matter how much she roughs it up. As scholar Claudrena Harold told me, "There's a way in which Mariah's singing is very digestible no matter how experimental it gets. And that's a very hard thing to do. That's something she got from Vanessa Bell Armstrong, who had brought live improvisation together with studio precision."[8] I'd also argue that Mariah belongs in a category with Minnie Riperton and Luther Vandross, two R&B legends who did not grow up singing in church choirs and, perhaps for that reason, developed vocal styles centered on nuances and dynamics that are easier to capture with high-end studio microphones than in a boisterous live environment.

Though overshadowed by the seasonal omnipresence of the more secular "All I Want for Christmas Is You," "Jesus Oh What a Wonderful Child" is the album's most important vocal performance. Mariah had rarely sounded so unfettered. Because of the climax-oriented structure of the pop ballads she was then known for, she often seemed tightly wound and laser-focused, like an archer concentrating on her target. "Jesus Oh What a Wonderful Child" complicates that persona by revealing her ability to dive in with musicians and jam, drawing on an improvisational art she describes in her memoir as "a miraculous madness."[9]

Mariah has an intuitive feel for how to fill up and decorate musical space. The background singers deliver the main melody as she reshapes each of their lines, creating a seesawing dynamic between choir and soloist, and illustrating her adeptness at gospel strategies of call-and-response. She dips and glides over the outro vamp, propelled to ever higher heights by a frenzied organ and tambourines. At one point, language itself begins to break down. Just as she did with the scats in the "Anytime You Need a Friend" remix, Mariah revels in rhythmic sounds with no denotative meaning, taking the first syllable of "Jesus" and quadrupling it over a staccato pattern, as if submitting to a glossolalic spasm. This trance-inducing repetition is a trademark of gospel, and Mariah proves herself well-schooled in the style by trying out the name "Jesus" in an array of melodic and melismatic configurations.

Religious music may strive for a universal, cosmic address, but its terms and conventions are often culturally insular. Assuming the guise of a gospel singer is not something most pop stars with no substantial background in the Black church can pull off. Despite the improvisational freedom it offers, the role demands a show not just of vocal power but of authenticity. By this point, Mariah had already faced a slew of think pieces about her mixed-race identity: in a *New York Times* article published the same year as the release of *Merry Christmas*, Michael Eric Dyson asked, "If she's not clearly black yet sings in a black style, is she singing black music? And what difference does it make?"[10] As such, Mariah was likely conscious of the racial dimensions of her gospel homage. The direct-from-the-pulpit testifying of "Jesus Oh What a Wonderful Child" implicitly asserts her belonging among Black women by grounding her in an idiom with which they are widely and readily associated.

Gospel has long engaged in a dialogue with popular music. In the 1970s and '80s, with the emergence of Edwin Hawkins, Andrae Crouch, the Winans, and other radio-friendly acts, the music incorporated the language of modern pop in ways that made it palatable to wider audiences. By the late '80s, Crouch had worked with Madonna, and BeBe and CeCe Winans had sung with Whitney Houston. And yet, while gospel was no stranger to crossover, major pop breakthroughs were rare. In the context of best-selling Christmas records, the influence of Black church music was, rather inexplicably, not a dominant one.

*Merry Christmas* can't take full credit for the sales boom of contemporary gospel in the late '90s — that wave of success, years in the making, would have come about without Mariah — but there *is* something striking about her consistent acknowledgment of the music's impact on her. She was perhaps ideally positioned to bring gospel to a broader public. With no formal allegiance to the Black Christian community, Mariah wasn't mired in some of the disputes that had arisen within the field at the end of the '80s, conflicts that split the genre into discernibly traditional and contemporary factions. She could integrate elements of gospel into a beat-driven track meant for the clubs (such as her collaborations with C+C Music Factory), but she could do so without fear of enduring the controversy that befell gospel legend Tramaine Hawkins, whose spiritually themed 1985 dance record "Fall Down" caused a stir among religious audiences. On the other hand, Mariah could make an earnest attempt at a traditional gospel sound and know that the majority of her non-Black and international listeners would not be knowledgeable enough about the music's history to measure her against its standards or to call her out for falling short.

Years after *Merry Christmas*, Mariah has continued to strengthen her connections with gospel. She is a well-studied disciple of the music; in her memoir, she mentions not just the most celebrated names but also the lesser-known '90s group Men of Standard. She has enlisted church-trained songwriters such as "Big Jim" Wright and Kenneth Crouch (nephew of Andraé Crouch) as key collaborators. She has featured the sermonizing of her pastor, the late Reverend Clarence Keaton, on two fiery album closers: "Fly Like a Bird," from 2005's *The Emancipation of Mimi*, and the Bible-quoting "I Wish You Well," from 2008's $E=MC^2$. And in one of the highlights on 2014's *Me. I Am Mariah . . . The Elusive Chanteuse*, she combined the contemporary gospel song "Can't Give Up Now," recorded by Mary Mary in 2010, with the 1978 James Cleveland classic "I Don't Feel No Ways Tired" — a brilliant, generation-bridging gesture that showed an insider's knowledge of the music's past and present.

Mariah isn't often credited with being a shape-shifter. Perhaps this is because her most profound transformations have materialized incrementally on a sonic level rather than as 180-degree turns of her celebrity image. And during her years of greatest prominence, her experimentation was happening mostly in the margins. By claiming house and gospel as zones of relative freedom, Mariah fostered a commitment to two kinds of music that held limited mass-market appeal. She was playing with sounds that most of her mainstream fans would not be curious or tuned-in enough to notice.

There's ambition, even hubris, in Mariah's genre adventures: in them, she's letting us know that a mind as restless as hers needs other realms in which to travel — realms vaster than the paradigmatic radio hit. At the same time, there's an aspect of service at play here. Mariah was beginning to address segments of her fanbase that, by and large, were as neglected and unseen as she had always felt.

I see in Mariah the spirit of the outsider, the skills of improvisation and adaptation born of having little sure footing in the world. And though I don't want to over-romanticize her artistic choices, I hear (or imagine) in them a gesture toward solidarity. Here she was, one of the world's most broadly appealing singers, and instead of flinging scraps of affection to her non-white, non-hetero fans, she was putting in the time to craft unique experiences for them that count among her best work.

Through my enjoyment of this music, I'm able to think through my own ambivalence toward the identities I inhabit as well as ones I've relinquished. In Mariah's club remixes, I hear a bygone era of queer culture that I never experienced or witnessed — one that seems more remote than it should and can only be revived in my imagination. Through her forays into gospel, I feel my own conflicted nostalgia for the Christianity of my youth, which comforted me with its message of a peace that "passeth all understanding" while also hurting me with its racism and homophobia. These associations are a lot to put on any one artist, but I think Mariah's music is strong enough to bear this weight.

The way Mariah blends into different cultural contexts may strike some as opportunistic. But for fans who share her experience of outsideness, there's something exhilarating about her path from mimicry to mastery. Her hunger to be embraced — to belong somewhere while at the same time staying true to herself — would become a powerful undercurrent in her relationship to the cutting edge of Black popular music. Rebranding herself for the urban contemporary market was not a stretch for her, because stylistic dexterity had been one of her most obvious assets from the beginning. Unlike house and gospel, though, R&B and hip-hop were hurtling toward the center of the mainstream in the mid-1990s, at a moment when Mariah was looking for a meaningful identity to call her own.

# 4

# OUT OF THE CHRYSALIS

I was nine years old the first time I noticed a Mariah Carey poster hanging in a store. It was a blown-up replica of the black-and-white cover of *Daydream*, the record she had just released — and the first album my family bought on CD. In that moment, the voice that had hypnotized me on the radio attached itself to an image that was just as entrancing. I still remember her big, airbrushed, lustrously smooth face peering down from the high perch on the wall, and the feeling of being dwarfed by its planetary presence.

If Mariah had been aiming to project the appearance of authority and confidence, she couldn't have done much better than enlisting influential *Vogue* photographer Steven Meisel, who had shot Madonna's *Like a Virgin* eleven years earlier. On that cover, Madonna is similarly pictured in monochrome, directing an imperious gaze at the camera. But unlike her, Mariah stands upright and statuesque in the *Daydream* album art, giving a power pose that accentuates the length of her body. The look is neither high-concept nor blatantly come-hither, and her outfit is austere to the point of being nondescript — a far cry from the summery plaid wardrobe she wore in the videos for "Emotions" and "Dreamlover." This isn't an entirely sexless image, though: the lower half of her shirt is unbuttoned, baring a triangle of stomach. It's an indication of burgeoning sensuality from an artist who, in contrast to Madonna, had often come across as an incurable Pollyanna.

I'm intrigued by the dissonance between Meisel's severe glamour shot and the reverie referred to in the title. Instead of evoking the warm-blooded emotions of the album's hit singles, Meisel's photograph introduces Mariah as a classic Hollywood-style ice queen who revels in being unreadable. The portrait seems meant to illustrate *Daydream*'s discordant final lyric—the last line of "Looking In," the biggest downer Mariah had ever written. This extroverted pop album—full of big sounds and sweeping gestures—closes with a sigh as aloof as the direct-to-camera glare on its cover: "They'll never know the real me."

Who was this real Mariah? There hadn't been much of a chance to get to know the woman—what her dreams and fears were, what made her tick—though her voice had permeated the airwaves throughout the previous half-decade. It wasn't always clear how she stood out from an increasingly crowded diva pack that included Whitney Houston (both singers could barely suppress a groan every time they were asked about each other in the press) and the increasingly prominent Céline Dion. And in a 1995 article in *Time* magazine, writer Christopher John Farley dismissed most of Mariah's output as "sugary and artificial—Nutrasweet soul."[1]

Most pop songs traffic in generalities and inanities, so why were critics eager to single out Mariah? Maybe because she had the trappings of a too-big-to-fail product: "no amount of quibbling is going to prevent Mariah from becoming bigger than the African continent,"[2] read one racist assessment in the British weekly *Melody Maker*. Or maybe people believed they were entitled to know more about her. Except for a few stray, up-by-the-bootstraps details in "Make It Happen," her lyrics were inoffensively universal, revealing nothing about her tough childhood on Long Island, New York, or her unhappy marriage. And though she had never hidden it, her racial identity was still subject to people's assumptions and ignorance. According to Michaela Angela Davis, who cowrote Mariah's memoir, "There was this narrative . . . in the collective imagination that Mariah did not identify as Black"[3]—either that she was trying to pass as white or that she wasn't Black at all.

*Village Voice* columnist Lisa Jones aired these suspicions in 1994 when she wrote:

> By marketing themselves as anything but black, do light-complexioned entertainers such as Carey become, in the eyes of most Americans, de facto whites? And do Carey and other people of color who feel more at ease representing themselves by their combination ethnic heritage, and not by race (making use of the privilege to remain outside), teach the world how to be "raceless"?[4]

To endure in the pop imagination, entertainers are under pressure to symbolize something that can be boiled down to a zeitgeist-friendly public relations pitch. But the lacunae of Mariah's life and art had combined to create a persona that signified nothing so much as its own elusiveness—what some perceived as an emotional and racial void. Yet despite her own inscrutable image, Mariah was well on her way to becoming an international icon. The era ushered in by that commanding *Daydream* photo came right on time, differentiating Mariah from her peers at a point when her status as a hitmaker was reliable enough to take for granted.

As with so much of Mariah's work, the discussion must begin with her voice. The mid-1990s confirmed her as a vocal singularity, a genius of singing who could no longer be dismissed as a mere physiological marvel or a pretender to someone else's throne. In retrospect, the moment feels even more precious because of what Mariah herself has noted about her finicky instrument. In a 1999 interview, she describes her voice as "bizarre" and "not standard," as if she were talking about a congenital abnormality. She explains that the complex harmonics in her tone are best captured by a PZM drum microphone capable of picking up the air flow in her vocal cords.[5] Elsewhere, she mentions that in medical lectures, her doctor refers to her as a freak specimen, and that touring requires her to implement unusually strict measures to rest her voice. Few pop stars have spoken of their vocal anatomy with this much specificity and self-awareness; indeed, few inspire this much curiosity about the subject. For superfans, this kind of analysis has the odd effect of both mythologizing her gift (perhaps not unlike how Italians once fetishized castrati) and demystifying it.

There are moments in some great singers' lives when the voice achieves an illusion of total elasticity, as though it were unencumbered by the laws of nature. A voice in this condition convinces you that it can do just about anything it wants; instead of being driven by the singer's will, it seems to possess a life all its own. Fans who know how Mariah's voice has changed through the years can hear this quality on *Daydream* and its 1997 follow-up, *Butterfly*. Our ears perk up at the paradox of something that's completely controlled yet unbridled.

Though this pair of albums tells an important story of her artistic evolution, when I reminisce about Mariah's voice in the mid-1990s I tend to think first of her live performances. Mariah didn't grow up singing in church like Whitney, or in piano bars like Céline. She has always preferred the privacy of the studio. In her memoir, she describes her desire for solitude, writing: "If I could do my own engineering, I would record like Prince and be completely alone."[6] During her early years in the spotlight, Mariah's stage presence was sometimes underwhelming, and her live vocals lacked the improvisational vigor of her house- and gospel-influenced material. Her shyness about the stage led to chatter, which in 1992 inspired a well-received *MTV Unplugged* set (later released as an EP) that proved she was no figment of studio trickery. But with so much scrutiny aimed at her live singing, she was understandably nervous and uneven during her first tour, which was launched to promote *Music Box*.

Footage of her concerts at Madison Square Garden and the Tokyo Dome during the 1996 *Daydream* world tour reveals a significant change. She's free in her body and doesn't seem concerned with having to prove herself. While she may not be attempting elaborate choreography (for Mariah, dancing never goes much further than a bending of the knees and a swaying of the hips), her energy is magnetic. She darts up and down the stage, gesticulates with abandon, loses herself in song. Seeing how her uninhibited movements correspond to the incomparable state of her voice, you can imagine how such bodily freedom must have translated in the studio sessions for *Daydream* and *Butterfly*, which captured a singer operating at the peak of her powers.

No one would teach anyone to sing this way, and no one is born with the innate ability to sing this way. Mariah's vocal style in the mid-1990s is the product of curiosity, exploration, and invention. It's hard to explain what's so bewitching about her vocals in this era without obsessing over the finest grains of detail. Her timbre here is a few shades lighter — less insistent, more angelic — with a slight, pleasant whininess that adds urgency to some of her phrasing. Perhaps it's this lighter touch that allowed her to bob and weave so nimbly through her five octaves, her tone remaining polished even as she executes extremely complicated, yodel-like transitions between registers, her pitch on point as she cuts unexpected paths up and down the scale. There's no trace of the tentative newbie or the overachieving try-hard. Like Sarah Vaughan in the '50s and Aretha Franklin in the '60s, she sounds as if she's flying.

When the skills required to perform any daunting physical feat have been mastered and internalized, the performer's focus can turn elsewhere — in Mariah's case, to matters of musical craft. *Daydream* was her best album yet, and despite being recorded at the breakneck pace that she was by then accustomed to (*Merry Christmas* had been released just a year prior), very little on it feels tossed off, a sign of maturity that helps it surpass its predecessors. The notion that albums should be coherent statements has usually been more strongly associated with rock, but Mariah must have been aware that one stellar LP could do wonders for a pop star's cachet. The specter of Michael Jackson's 1982 masterpiece *Thriller* loomed large, and female R&B acts that funneled their artistic ambitions into the format — including, in 1994, Mary J. Blige with *My Life* and TLC with *CrazySexyCool* — earned the kind of critical acclaim that had eluded Mariah.

*Daydream* may not be quite as cohesive or daring as those records, but it's a wonderfully smooth listen from start to finish. Still, the album existed in global consciousness less as a unified whole than as a string of three monster hits, each of which demonstrated Mariah's individuality while highlighting her knack for fusing other sounds with her own. Mariah had been honing her chameleonic skills on her remixes, so it's fitting that the cultural significance of *Daydream*'s lead single hinges on yet another demographically targeted reinvention — this time with a grimy hip-hop twist.

"Fantasy" is built on a looped excerpt of Tom Tom Club's 1981 "Genius of Love," a daffy mix of funk, rap, and reggae by a white band (consisting of two members of Talking Heads) tipping its hat to a slew of Black influences: George Clinton, Bootsy Collins, and Kurtis Blow are among the many luminaries name-checked in the lyrics. Perhaps Mariah was cognizant of the fact that the song represented something of a bridge between white and Black musical milieus, and also that its opening line — "What you gonna do when you get out of jail?" — echoed the sense of imprisonment she was experiencing in her marriage. She suggested "Genius of Love," a childhood favorite of hers, to producer Dave "Jam" Hall as a possible element to build a track around. The idea piggybacked on the sample-based approach of their previous collaboration,

"Dreamlover," and just like that record's use of the Emotions' "Blind Alley" — a song famously sampled by rapper Big Daddy Kane — the choice of "Genius of Love" was a wink at hip-hop heads.

In its infancy, hip-hop freely intermingled with new wave and other popular genres of the '80s; Tom Tom Club's link to the rap scene serves as a case in point. "Genius of Love" became legendary as a favorite source text for MCs, spawning remakes such as Dr. Jeckyll & Mr. Hyde's "Genius Rap" and Grandmaster Flash and the Furious Five's "It's Nasty." Mariah and Hall were drawing on a well-established tradition, one that would have been apparent to anyone who had been observing the latest innovations in Black music.

At the time "Fantasy" was released, sampling had only started becoming a trend less than a decade earlier, when the first affordable sampler machines hit the market and made looping easy, giving birth to tracks such as the 1987 Eric B. and Rakim song "I Know You Got Soul," which spliced together fragments from classic funk records. As Mariah's use of this technique developed in the years to come, it became clear that she viewed it not as a musical garnish but as an act of curation and connoisseurship. Unlike most of her peers, few of whom shared her expertise as a producer, she regularly drew on references to songs she grew up listening to. These included the work of R&B stars from the '80s who never made a huge impact in the pop market, such as Stacy Lattisaw, Loose Ends, and DeBarge. This is one reason why, for R&B fans, Mariah's music from 1995 onward feels so rooted in the genre: her quotational style turns contemporary R&B history — not the prestigious soul records so dear to the boomer generation, but more recent, less canonical fare — into a dazzling hall of mirrors.

The album version of "Fantasy," the track that most of the world would have heard on top-forty radio, is as tenacious an earworm as anything Mariah has ever made. Part of the song's magic lies in how it converts an odd bricolage of sounds, centered on the friction between the singer's ethereal voice and the sample's quacking synth groove, into something so intuitive and organic it doesn't feel contrived. But it's the Bad Boy remix, produced by Puff Daddy, that transformed "Fantasy" from a pop ditty into a hip-hop monument. Besides stripping the record down to its skeleton, Puff Daddy doesn't do a lot of retooling, and he didn't have to: the idea of goody-goody Mariah in a pas de deux with Wu-Tang Clan member Ol' Dirty Bastard (ODB), who was notorious for his run-ins with the law, is enough to flip the tune's "images of rapture" on their head. Rubbing up against ODB's hilariously sloppy lyrics and drunk-clown drawl, Mariah's belts and trills sound wacky and incongruous. Regardless of whether she was conscious of it, you get the sense that she was undercutting her hegemonic vocal power by embracing someone who could spit in the face of all that her voice had come to symbolize: beauty, discipline, precision, mass appeal.

In the years since, the Bad Boy remix of "Fantasy" has been touted as one of the first major collaborations between a pop singer and a rapper. This is a slightly misleading exaggeration: in 1989, Jody Watley had enlisted Eric B. and Rakim for her song "Friends," which hit Number 9 on the pop charts. A year later, Glenn Medeiros's "She Ain't Worth It," featuring a rap verse by Bobby Brown, went to Number 1. But there is a reason people remember

"Fantasy" as a groundbreaking collision of two worlds: it collapsed the hierarchy perpetuated by pop's risk-averse overlords. The spectacle of a world-famous star going out of her way to tarnish her image by associating with an outlandish, foul-mouthed renegade was an unforgettable provocation, one that made a mockery of the prejudices that attach to musical categories — and one that Mariah pulls off with sly insouciance.

What the "Fantasy" remix should be remembered for is the way Mariah invites herself into the realm of hard-core rap while also toying with people's presumptuous, racially loaded ideas about whether she belonged there. ODB's appearance wasn't exactly out of the blue; the 1993 Wu-Tang Clan song "Da Mystery of Chessboxin'" contains an affectionate reference to the diva ("I set the microphone on fire / rap styles vary / and carry like Mariah"). Nor was this a case of a pop princess opportunistically or ignorantly copying someone's style. In a 1996 cover story in *Vibe* magazine, Puff Daddy says that Mariah's desire to feature ODB "bugged [him] out" initially, until he realized that she "had a real passion for hip-hop — even for the edgier stuff that a cynic might accuse her of dabbling in only to enhance her street credibility."[7]

In the same article, Mariah says, "It wasn't like I said, 'Tell me, who does good remixes?' or 'Who's the hot rapper of the moment?' I knew what I wanted to do and who I wanted to do it with."[8]

Though Mariah has thrown the spotlight on many rappers over the years (including pioneering female MCs such as Da Brat, who delivers some of her best bars in Mariah's songs), she has less frequently passed the mic to singers of her caliber. On the rare occasion that she does, the unique qualities of her voice, offset by other tones and styles, become that much easier to appreciate. On *Daydream*'s second single — an elegy for the dead called "One Sweet Day" — she shares the spotlight with Boyz II Men, one of the decade's most talented R&B groups. There's so much happening in the vocals — especially at the key-changing climax, when Mariah's upper register sails across Boyz II Men's rich, bottom-heavy four-part blend — that all the potential corniness of the lyrics is burned away in a blaze of sonic profusion. As the singers' highs and lows spin around one another, it's as if their voices are measuring the distance between heaven and earth.

While no instrument in pop has more layers and textures than Mariah's, one voice on its own can never replicate the joys of two or more locking into harmony. It's a pleasure to hear Mariah finding community among other vocalists, as she would later do with worthy peers such as Whitney Houston and Brian McKnight. (On occasion, she's even been willing to hover in the background of other artists' songs, as she does to enchanting effect in Babyface's "Every Time I Close My Eyes" and Allure's "All Cried Out.") It's particularly exciting to hear her as one of five powerful voices, all tasked with nailing their steps in an intricate choreography of harmonies, countermelodies, and riffs. "One Sweet Day" makes clear that, consummate soloist though she is, Mariah would have been no less incredible as a member of a group.

Along with "Always Be My Baby," a superb first collaboration with Atlanta producer Jermaine Dupri and songwriting partner Manuel Seal, these *Daydream* songs were everywhere that year. ("One Sweet Day" enjoyed a record-breaking sixteen weeks at the top of the Hot 100.)

At the time, I was a kid in Kuala Lumpur, where my family lived for a period, and it's partly through the prism of these songs that I can recall that year so vividly. In a world that seemed to me devoid of certainty and familiarity, Mariah's music offered those things.

It wasn't just that her voice was as much a part of the atmosphere as the daily prayers broadcast from our neighborhood mosque, or that she was as much an emblem of American glory as Elvis had been for my father when he was growing up in Malaysia in the 1950s and '60s. And it wasn't just that the more I heard these songs, the more I craved to hear them again—a desire that flung me into a state of anticipation every time the radio came on in the car, and every time I heard the top-forty station in a restaurant or shopping center.

I think there was something else going on: my sentimental education. "Fantasy" was a gust of euphoria, as strong as any high I'd ever felt. "One Sweet Day" had me fighting back tears. And "Always Be My Baby" was something in between; it's one of the first times Mariah had constructed a song that unspools like a string of distinct but equally catchy hooks, and yet all that jubilant melody-making hides an undercurrent of sourness ("when your days and your nights get a little bit colder," Mariah sings, wagging a finger at a departing lover). That these three experiences emanated from the mysterious woman on that poster in the record store taught me something about how close happiness was to sadness, and how interchangeable these emotions often are in the language of music, since both can lead to the same ecstasy.

For me, *Daydream*'s three major singles are still inseparable from the sugar rush I'd get every time I encountered them in public. Each instance was as exciting as a chance encounter with a crush. In much the same way that Mariah's samples create a map of the music that was totemic for her in childhood, her best-loved hits from this period form a palimpsest of the life I was living between two continents. These days, whenever I hear one of these songs playing at the grocery store or blasting from a car outside my Brooklyn apartment, I stop what I'm doing. I could be eating out with a friend, and the conversation will immediately come to a halt. I can't help it. I'm unglued from time, transported back to that stretch of months in 1995 and '96, when this music was the center of my emotional world.

For many who came of age in the '90s, the idea of a universally shared pop consciousness went hand in hand with the era's feel-good multiculturalism. United Colors of Benetton was running its iconic, racially diverse ad campaigns. Sitcoms with all-Black casts, such as *The Fresh Prince of Bel-Air* and *Family Matters*, were widely embraced. And Black artists were so prevalent on the Hot 100 that there was an outward appearance that integration, at least in the realm of entertainment, had finally been achieved. Growing up, I didn't know about the days when Black artists had to hope and pray to get into rotation on MTV, the days when the biggest records on urban radio often went unheard by most Americans. Things had changed so much by the end of the century that, in the year *Daydream* was released, fourteen of *Billboard*'s top twenty pop hits were songs that had also landed on the R&B/Hip-Hop chart.

But if R&B was at the heart of popular music — in a way that was more far-reaching than even the civil-rights-era renaissance of Motown and Stax — why didn't the distinction between R&B and pop cease to matter? And why have so many musicians (including non-Black ones) had the urge to associate themselves with R&B instead of with its presumably more all-embracing sibling?

In his study of music-genre formation, *Categorizing Sound*, scholar David Brackett charts the drama that has trailed the labeling and relabeling of Black popular music over the years. What began as "rhythm and blues" — a catch-all term for "almost any music that is preferred by most Negroes,"[9] in the words of *Billboard* columnist and radio personality Bill Gavin — became, in the mid-1960s, "soul," a term that underscored the centrality of African American identity and political conscience to the genre. Then, in the early '80s, *Billboard* began calling its Soul category "Black music" to honor the heterogeneity of what was appearing on the chart. At around the same time, the controversial phrase "urban contemporary" was coming into common usage as a de-racialized alternative that could attract advertisers uninterested in audiences of color. The ambivalences underlying all these name changes are bound up with the thorny question of how much race should determine the boundaries we draw around certain sounds — sounds that can't even be relied on to remain cleanly delineated from one another.

While there are few satisfying answers in this ongoing debate, history reminds us of a persistent truth: that there's nothing neutral about music, that it operates within the power structures and cultural norms that shape what gets made and how we interpret it. Born out of racial symbolism, R&B is, according to critic Kelefa Sanneh, "a genre that can never quite decide whether it wants to be the universal sound of young (and not-so-young) America, or Black people's best-kept secret, or — somehow — both at once."[10]

Owing to a confluence of factors—her mixed-race heritage, her cross-cultural tastes, the money machine that secured her omnipresence—Mariah has been able to occupy the realms of pop and R&B like few artists before or since. This has made her a conduit through which the latter could become a global lingua franca. But to the extent that one can be faithful to such an amorphous and loosely defined concept, Mariah has also stayed true to what R&B means to its most passionate devotees, who see it as something to be held sacred, separate from the homogenized pop field into which it has often been subsumed. And as she began to insist on her status as an R&B artist, it seemed that she was implicitly arguing for her right to be seen as a Black woman.

Mariah knows that R&B (and its link to the spiritual, racial concept of soul) has a specific resonance for many listeners. She also knows it's a profound legacy upon which to build her own, one that puts her in the company of the artists she grew up loving. As she once told critic Touré, "Pop is not a genre."[11] At a certain point, aligning with a category untethered from any identity or community must have been like consigning her music to meaninglessness.

Far more than her previous albums, *Daydream* shows how sharply attuned Mariah was to R&B's past and future. She was associating with some of the genre's key players—moguls at the helm of successful urban-music brands (Babyface, who cowrote the heavenly ballad "Melt Away," had cofounded LaFace in 1989; Puff Daddy and Dupri had launched Bad Boy and So So Def, respectively, in 1993). At the same time, she was taking care to create R&B of a sort no longer in fashion.

Nestled between "Fantasy" and "One Sweet Day" on

the album's track list is the underappreciated "Underneath the Stars," and it's no less a treasure than those singles, or the quiet-storm records whose spirit it summons. Like that peek-a-boo of belly button on the *Daydream* artwork, the song is also something of an erotic tease. Thanks to a chiffon-soft vocal, a sparkling instrumental built on a Fender Rhodes keyboard (a quintessential ingredient of vintage soul), and Mariah's most vivid, carefully wrought lyrics to date, this ode to young love plays like a secret whispered in the dark by one R&B fan to another. Where most of *Daydream*'s standout tracks show Mariah's eagerness to bring her sound up to date, "Underneath the Stars" demonstrates that she also knows that the splendor of modern Black music does not rest solely in its chart potential or on its cutting edge.

*Butterfly*, the album that decisively reintroduced Mariah as an R&B artist, was recorded at a time of upheaval in her personal life. The woman who confessed to depression at the end of *Daydream* ("She smiles through a thousand tears / and harbors adolescent fears") was now separated from the husband who had aided her ascent. In her memoir, Mariah describes several incidents that illustrate how monstrously paranoid Tommy Mottola could be, including a time when she and Da Brat stole away to Burger King to get French fries in the middle of recording the hip-hop remix of "Always Be My Baby," only to find themselves handled like fugitives by a swarm of security personnel upon their return.[12] "He rolled over me like a fog," Mariah writes about Mottola. "His presence felt dense and oppressive. He was like humidity — inescapable."[13] Freeing herself from that nightmare, Mariah wanted to call the shots in her art too.

This narrative of captivity and self-liberation serves as the premise of the video for *Butterfly*'s lead single, "Honey" (another first-rate Puff Daddy coproduction, built on a sample of the Treacherous Three's "The Body Rock" provided by the rapper Q-Tip). In this Paul Hunter–directed mini-movie, Mariah stars as an abducted secret agent who jumps off the balcony of a mansion into a swimming pool, emerges in a skimpy bathing suit inspired by that of Ursula Andress in *Dr. No*, and gets pursued by men on jet skis. As has been the case for so many other female pop stars (Madonna and Janet Jackson before Mariah, Britney Spears and Christina Aguilera after her), personal autonomy is telegraphed in a slinky, sexed-up image. The newly single diva was packaging herself as flirty, fleshy, and a lot more fun than anyone had previously imagined.

Since Mariah's debut in 1990, hip-hop had gone from being perceived by some as a temporary phenomenon (early on, *Billboard* had dismissed it as a "passing novelty that will soon go the way of all fads")[14] to being recognized as a vital art form and a multimillion-dollar industry that drew in young audiences of all races. Rap was now mass culture. MTV and pop radio, which not too long before had been the preserve of white lite-rock acts such as Bryan Adams and Bon Jovi, had assimilated rap into their mix of mainstream hits, opening swaths of programming time for various styles and subgenres to thrive. Pop radio had not been this racially integrated since the early '70s.

Unlike much of what had been considered pop music in the previous decade, rap had acquired connotations of real-world danger. In the years leading up to *Butterfly*'s 1997 release, the "gangsta" strain of the genre had become the subject of congressional hearings and bipartisan cries of obscenity. And earlier in 1997, the Notorious B.I.G. —

the most lionized MC in Puff Daddy's stable of Bad Boy artists, who had mentioned Mariah in his 1994 song "Just Playing (Dreams)" — was murdered in a drive-by shooting.

Like the racial and sexual controversies ignited by the emergence of rock and roll in the '50s, the uproar over hip-hop only intensified its appeal among young listeners. According to scholar Tricia Rose, "No black musical form before hip hop — no matter how much it 'crossed over' into mainstream American culture — ever attracted the level of corporate attention and mainstream media visibility, control, and intervention that characterizes hip hop today."[15] Thanks to *Vibe* magazine and publications like it, the perception of R&B was also changing. Instead of being a fusty, out-of-touch elder incompatible with the new sounds on the block, the music was reenvisioned as an important part of the "hip-hop nation," a now fully corporatized marketing regime that dictated what was cool and *real* in all areas of youth culture. Urban radio playlists were now split between R&B and rap, and the two genres, once diametrically opposed, were starting to blend into each other.[16]

The intersection of this industry shift with Mariah's personal metamorphosis made *Butterfly* possible, but ultimately that's not what earns it an all-important position within Mariah's discography. Rather, it's the slipperiness of the music itself, which at times is so sensuous that it seems to disregard the tense conditions under which it was made. Mariah had always been a detail-oriented perfectionist in the studio, with strong ideas about sounds other than her own voice, but no one would have thought to describe her as subtle. With *Butterfly*, though, she was making music that thrived on nuance, that invited listeners to put on their headphones and pay microscopic attention to the layers beneath the surface. Even in the moments when she's purging her sorrows and resentments, *Butterfly* often plays like an intimate sound bath. She has written that producing the album was "the beginning of another level in my healing process."[17]

Walter Afanasieff had been the man behind several of Mariah's biggest hits, but for reasons that have never been fully disclosed, their relationship was fraying beyond repair. *Butterfly* is the final Mariah album on which he is listed as a major contributor. His adult-contemporary style—which the singer now considers a vestige of Mottola's stifling vision for her career—gets its last hurrah in "Butterfly," "My All," and "Whenever You Call," three ballads that replicate the same song structure and sentiment everyone had come to expect from their collaborations. These are some of the most sophisticated and deeply felt compositions the pair ever wrote together, with transcendent vocals to match. But if these songs come off as minor triumphs in the context of the album, it's because the hip-hop cuts showcase Mariah's voice doing things that we hadn't heard it do before.

Coproduced by the Trackmasters, "The Roof (Back in Time)" offers the first indication of a new direction. It kicks off with a cinematically ominous piano riff soon accompanied by a throbbing hip-hop beat, spookily chiming bells lifted from the 1984 Run-D.M.C. song "Rock Box," and Mariah's wispy vocals. The track's rhythmic foundation is derived from Mobb Deep's 1995 "Shook Ones, Part II," marking the first time Mariah sampled a piece of music that had been released so recently. And just as the original song brought the hellscape of Queensbridge street crime to life in vérité detail, so too was Mariah attempting something documentary-like — or at least as close to reportage as she'd ever come.

"Shook Ones, Part II" had been playing on the car radio during a ride back from a steamy evening she spent with baseball star Derek Jeter.[18] Like Mariah, Jeter is mixed-race, and the two formed a brief but powerful connection not long after her split from Mottola. Upon hearing "Shook Ones, Part II" that night, she rushed to write lyrics on top of the beat, immortalizing the feelings of lust and longing she'd experienced as if they were a storm brewing on the horizon: "It wasn't raining yet / but it was definitely / a little misty on that warm November night . . ." Mariah had rarely been so carnal, and she'd certainly never made sexual desire sound so menacing or lonely. The song narrates the play-by-play of her and Jeter's rendezvous, but it's framed as a Proustian memento. The heroine is doomed to latch on to the memory "every time [she] feels the need," and the song is the vehicle returning her to the site of passion.

In keeping with the evanescent tone of the lyrics, Mariah brings a level of delicacy to her vocal that's remarkable for hip-hop singing. She delivers her lines in a sultry, almost mumbly coo (what she calls her "whisper register"), a sound that would be her signature in the decades to come. In addition, the tightly stacked background vocals by Kelly Price and Mariah give the track a three-dimensional heft and an alluring femininity that counters the disquieting, macho beat.

Mariah's apprenticeship as a background singer had predisposed her to pay attention to harmonies and arrangements; in her memoir, she writes that while singing with veterans such as Cindy Mizelle, she "began to discover how to create nuances and textures in vocal arrangements and how to use my voice to build layers, like a painter."[19] It's on *Butterfly* where the line between background and foreground is at its blurriest. Each vocal track becomes its own detour into the past, pulling us further away from the present tense of the lead performance. In the same way that funk was born when the rhythmic components of R&B were placed front and center, the brand of contemporary R&B that Mariah helped popularize threw the spotlight on harmony, countermelody, and ornamentation, making elements once considered secondary just as important as a song's main melody.

Multitrack recording had been popular since the 1960s, when the Beach Boys, Phil Spector, and Harry Nilsson recognized the technology's ability to juxtapose and blend multiple sonic elements. But while female R&B singers as different as Chaka Khan and Janet Jackson had made ambitious use of it before, the technique wasn't widespread in the world of diva pop, where a crisp, cleanly audible lead vocal was often treated as paramount. In a 2022 interview with *Rolling Stone*, Mariah recalled that background vocals had become so central to her creative process during the making of *Butterfly* that she preferred to record them before the lead, building out an atmosphere from exquisite filigree and pointillist detail.[20] Like Marvin Gaye in the '70s, Mariah sounds as if she's inviting us into her inner dialogue. She's singing to hear and soothe herself, and to speak back to her own train of thought. This background-forward aesthetic has gone on to inform some of the most innovative pop singing of the past quarter century, including the influential, densely layered vocals of R&B star Brandy.

A more jagged, high-strung side of Mariah's hip-hop singing makes its first appearance on "Breakdown,"

*Butterfly*'s gutsiest track. Where the new jack swing generation of R&B vocalists had incorporated hip-hop into their
music by riding atop its rhythms, Mariah took this stylistic
evolution one step further by mimicking the rat-a-tat flow
of rappers — specifically, Bone Thugs-n-Harmony. A year
earlier, the group had scored a pop hit with "Tha Cross-
roads," a foreboding meditation on mortality (in some
ways, a perfect companion piece to "One Sweet Day") in
which the lyrics are melodic but delivered in a staccato,
rap-like double time. And in the spring of 1997, Mariah
had fallen in love with the group's collaboration with the
Notorious B.I.G., in "Notorious Thugs." In "Breakdown,"
she adopts their cadence and applies it to a post-breakup
lament, and alongside two of the group's members (Krayzie
Bone and Wish Bone), she has no trouble keeping pace.

It's a power move, proving that she can hang with some
of the fastest-spitting MCs of the era, but "Breakdown"
contains real vulnerability too. As Mariah skitters anx-
iously through the chorus, nailing its twisty tempo and
mouthfuls of syllables, she sounds like someone dancing
as fast as she can to avoid having to stop and face reality,
hitting her marks so perfectly that no one would suspect
she's anything less than fine. In the closing minute and a
half, the chorus repeats like a mantra, a new set of ad-libs
piled on in each iteration, one more veil to keep the truth
at bay. At this point, the song has gotten so tightly wound
it might be the only thing keeping the singer from emotional collapse.

*Butterfly* is an act of rebellion, but a subdued one, freighted
with doubt and indeterminacy. The title track confronts
Mariah's toxic marriage at an odd remove; she casts herself

in the role of her own abuser, delivering words of wisdom and compassion she wishes Mottola could have offered her: "I have learned that beauty has to flourish in the light. / Wild horses run unbridled or their spirit dies." The songs about sex and romance float in a haze of unquenched longing and anxiety-ridden attachment. Repeatedly, Mariah takes stock of everything that can't be counted on, weighing whether the feelings she has romanticized are being reciprocated. This fixation on impermanent, unreliable love turns up even in the one cover on the album, Prince's "The Beautiful Ones," a song about erotic insecurity that she and the R&B group Dru Hill perform glacially, as if in a somnambulant trance.

The instability in the lyrics is echoed in the restlessness of Mariah's musical choices. If she'd been aiming to prove she could hang with a more rugged, masculine crowd, she hinted as much by demonstrating her fluency in the sounds of Mobb Deep and Bone Thugs. At the same time, this is an album of decadent beauty and rococo adornments. In track after track, Mariah leans into her most feminine vocal gestures; her tone is lighter than spun sugar, her melismatic runs like a winged creature's trajectory through the air, never settling for very long in any one place.

Mariah's greatest album is a portrait of someone who's made a home for herself in the in-between, someone who is, in her own words, "neither here nor there." But amid *Butterfly*'s ambivalences and contradictions lies a kind of certainty too — the confidence of an artist who knows she's finally making the music of her dreams.

# 5

# BETWEEN LAUGHTER AND LAMENT

Show business is strewn with authenticity claims. Through them, artists drum up fanfare for their reinventions, touting the freedoms that will allow them to put their art first, commercial pressures be damned. Mariah Carey was at such a turning point in the *Butterfly* era: in the press, her separation from Tommy Mottola served as a declaration of independence; in the music, her embrace of an urban Black aesthetic she felt had been suppressed and underpromoted on her previous albums offered the hope of a more uncompromising vision. Still, it wasn't clear how this "realer" Mariah would evolve, or what confidences and intimacies fans could expect her to go on sharing with them.

In the years that followed, a new image of Mariah began to emerge between two opposing temperaments. Her art became no less dialectically driven than that of R&B icons before her, such as Marvin Gaye and Al Green, but where those artists had been preoccupied with reconciling the soul and the flesh, she found herself on a different battleground, striving to find balance between melancholia and levity, depth and surface, the urge to wallow and the impulse to laugh off life's trials.

The average listener hadn't thought of Mariah as depressive (and her disclosure of her longtime struggle with bipolar disorder wouldn't be revealed for two decades).

If you grew up with Mariah in the '90s, you knew her as she was portrayed in magazines and on TV — including in music videos she directed herself, such as those for "Fantasy" and "Always Be My Baby." She was the girl frolicking in a field of flowers, the girl on rollerblades at the amusement park, the girl perched on a tire swing over a twilit lake. Disseminated at the height of her fame, these images locked her into a reverie of youth, one that she has helped extend well into her fifties. (As lambs know, "eternally twelve"[1] is one of her favorite self-descriptors.)

But even if her childhood struggles were seldom discussed in the press, Mariah had lived through plenty of hardship, and by the end of the '90s she was less hesitant about airing her grievances. As sure as she was about her talent, she was becoming equally convinced of another fact: that she'd been wronged for much of her life by those who were supposed to love her. She had disclosed these misfortunes in "Looking In," "Close My Eyes," and "Outside," deep cuts that made *Daydream* and *Butterfly* her most intimate albums to date. But the handful of confessional songs released in the years since have even darker shades; in them, you hear pop wielded as an instrument of personal justice — a platform for retribution. The lyrics make clear she isn't referring to some generalized miasma of sorrow but to actual and specific perpetrators she had to expunge from her inner circle.

Take, for example, the sneering bridge of "Petals," a song from 1999: "So many I considered closest to me / turned on a dime and sold me out dutifully." We know now, from her memoir, that these lines refer to family members who benefited from her financial support without having her best interests at heart.[2] Leap forward in time, and you'll

find this accusatory tone in 2008's "Side Effects," a chron-
icle of the emotional abuse she endured in her marriage,
in which Mariah describes "wakin' up scared some nights,
still dreamin' 'bout them violent times." It's there again in
2018's "Portrait," where she laments being "haunted by
those severed ties, pushing past the parasites."

If that last reference to bloodsucking organisms sounds
like something on a punk or grunge record, there's precedent for that. Unbeknownst to most, Mariah spent the mid-
1990s listening to hard rock and took an interest in bands
like Hole, Green Day, Sleater-Kinney, and L7. During the
making of *Daydream*, she secretly improvised a side project inspired by their music called *Someone's Ugly Daughter*,
ultimately released under the name Chick, a group fronted
by former roommate Clarissa Hughes.[3] The album cover,
which Mariah helped art-direct, mixes squalor with cheap
glamour in one crudely Photoshopped image of a dead
cockroach and a tube of lipstick. Though the project (all
but forgotten until she began talking about it publicly in
2020) was undertaken as a lark, one wonders what might
have happened if she had allowed herself to cultivate that
middle-finger attitude. At the same time, it's worth not-
ing that some of her most confrontational lyrics are not so
divergent in spirit from the angst peddled by those bands.
Beneath Mariah's beautiful vocals, you'll occasionally hear
an artist who can be bitter to the point of abjection.

When I listen to those rare instances when Mariah
sticks the knife in her enemies, I think not of the trium-
phant, chest-thumping divas with whom she is typically
categorized, but of a tradition of singer-songwriters
known for their vindictiveness: Marvin Gaye haranguing
his estranged first wife in *Here, My Dear*, for instance,

or Taylor Swift skewering her ex-lovers on record after record. Unlike these artists, Mariah was not widely recognized as the mind behind her own material, and her accounts of betrayal were never released as singles or prioritized on any album's track list, limiting their audience to ardent fans who delight in reading between the lines. But it's thanks to the existence of these songs that the lambs sensed a storm brewing in Mariah's life well before the broader public did.

In addition to stray hints in her music, Mariah started leaving audio messages on her website in the late '90s, a ritual that anticipated the rise of social media and turned her followers into confidants. Most of these messages were lighthearted, but in a few you could hear a mounting desperation, culminating in July 2001, when she exhaustedly declared, "I just can't trust anybody anymore right now because I don't understand what's going on."[4] Alarming as such flashes of transparency were, they fostered devotion, raising diehards — the ones who have the lyrics to "Outside" committed to memory or even tattooed on their bodies — above fair-weather fans.

This extreme vulnerability was also coming into view in high-profile media appearances. In 1999, she and her mother went on *The Oprah Winfrey Show* to discuss Mariah's experiences as a mixed-race child. For much of the show, Mariah looks more forlorn and sheepish than she ever had in such a public forum. She listens quietly as her mother, Patricia, recounts marrying Mariah's Black and Venezuelan American father in 1960 (seven years before interracial marriage became fully legal in the US) and the horrors that ensued: Patricia's rejection by her Irish Catholic parents, the indignities of housing discrimination, the poisoning of the Careys' family dog by a racist in their predominantly white neighborhood.

Winfrey tells Mariah, "My impression, based upon your skin color or even hearing you were biracial, is that you would have had this perfectly wonderful life . . . I never would have imagined you felt like an outcast."[5] It must have been frustrating to hear these assumptions so frankly articulated on national TV. No matter how many times Mariah had explained her racial identity since the beginning of her career, her Black heritage never failed to take some people by surprise and to inspire seemingly willful misunderstandings. To be recognized by the masses as a Black woman (and to avoid the accusation that she was appropriating Black culture), she had to engage in public spectacles of disclosure. But in submitting herself to scrutiny, she was also shouldering the burden of representing a stigmatized community, the members of which had long been reduced to an archetype, that of the "tragic mulatto."

For listeners intent on projecting their own turmoil onto the singers they love, any whiff of trauma can inspire passionate, sometimes masochistic identification. This is the case with male rockers like Kurt Cobain, and it's also true in the land of diva worship. In her classic novel *Sleepless Nights*, Elizabeth Hardwick fetishistically describes Billie Holiday's voice as "leaving a sort of scar of longing never satisfied, almost a wound of feeling."[6] Scholar Richard Dyer, examining the origins of Judy Garland's massive gay fanbase, finds the star's queer appeal in a "particular register of intense, authentic feeling . . . a combination of strength and suffering, and precisely the one in the face of the other."[7] A faithful student of diva history, Mariah must have been aware of this tradition, and of the fact that she didn't fit neatly into it; she wasn't anyone's idea of a tragic figure, at least not yet. By speaking about her struggles, she wasn't just shedding the demure persona that had made her so marketable to middle America; she was also, perhaps consciously, solidifying her bond with marginalized audiences—those fans who could intuitively empathize with her feelings of alienation and stories of survival.

It doesn't diminish the sincerity of her anguish (or her right to share it with us) to suggest that these revelations became a kind of currency for her. They made her more compelling than she had previously been, chipping away at the notion that she was born privileged. Where she was once fastidiously manicured and prudishly styled, now she was free to be rougher and more brittle around the edges.

Still, there were moments when you could see her falling back on the habits of pop-princess propriety. While "Looking In" and "Petals" exposed her resentments in diaristic fashion, more often she navigated between thinly veiled self-pity and the semblance of joie de vivre expected of a female star at the top of her game, never quite settling into either mood. You can detect this mix of emotions in her acceptance speech at the 1999 Billboard Music Awards, where she took home the prize for Artist of the Decade. With a grin on her face and arms outstretched, Mariah proclaimed, "I am not Cinderella. My life has *not* been a fairy tale."[8] Fans who had already been interpreting her signals of distress since the mid-1990s could choose to hear in those words either an exclamation of triumph over adversity or the sound of an ax being ground.

I remember what it was like to be a preteen fan and not know what to make of this duality, especially when the scales tipped in favor of the frothy and superficial. Such is the vibe on *Rainbow*, the 1999 follow-up to *Butterfly*. The album cover is pure bubblegum, down to the color scheme. In a wink to gay fans, Mariah enlisted the aggressively kitschy David LaChapelle to take her portrait, and the results were notably distinct from the smoldering looks and monochrome palette of *Daydream* and *Butterfly*. LaChapelle shot the singer like a pin-up, in a bosom-hugging white top and briefs, thighs smooth and waxy as Barbie-doll plastic, a rainbow radiating across her chest. Director Brett Ratner, who had recently scored a hit with the action-comedy *Rush Hour*, helmed the video for the infectious lead single, "Heartbreaker" (featuring Jay-Z), turning it into an occasion for zany set pieces. For the price of $2 million — one of the biggest budgets in music-video history — viewers were treated to cartoon interstitials, a cameo by Jerry O'Connell, and Mariah doing double duty as a teen-seeming version of herself and a brunette nemesis named Bianca.

The high-school ambiance of the "Heartbreaker" video (and its wardrobe centerpiece: faded jeans with the waistband ripped off) suggested that Mariah, now at the end of her twenties in a field where ageism was known to snuff out women's careers, was clinging to her youthfulness as the pop-culture ground shifted beneath her feet. Britney Spears had made her debut on the charts that January, and teen pop had conquered MTV. The pressure to jump on the bandwagon may be the only reasonable explanation why the B-list boy bands 98 Degrees and Westlife were brought in as Mariah's duet partners in this era; if her virtuosity risked making her seem stuffy and grown-up, these young men's vocal mediocrity might have been just what was needed to tamp down her pyrotechnics. Even Mariah's delightfully florid diction, by then a trademark of her songwriting style, could be understood as a part of the album's juvenile tone. Heard in this context, "incessantly" and "relinquish" (from "Heartbreaker") and "unvarnished" (from the second single, "Thank God I Found You"), sound like the vocabulary of someone cramming for the SAT.

Maybe it's a reflection of preadolescent fickleness that *Rainbow* had me doubting my favorite diva so soon after she'd won my young heart. But there was something legitimately deflating about my first encounters with the album. Where the music on *Butterfly* was fresh, expressive, and lovingly finessed, *Rainbow* felt haphazard and disconcertingly lax; though I didn't know this at the time, the album had been made in three months, in Mariah's haste to end her Sony contract.[9] It was as if her newfound flightiness, born of an apparent desire for freedom, meant she couldn't commit to any sound that might leave an impression that was too lasting. Formulaic or overly familiar choices crop up throughout the record. For instance, the main hook of "Heartbreaker" sounds like a close cousin of the "Dreamlover" chorus. Meanwhile, Mariah's former adult-contemporary partner Walter Afanasieff is swapped out for schlockmeister Diane Warren, whose two ballad contributions ("Can't Take That Away" and "After Tonight") are plodding and generic. And the more ambitious tracks (the five-minute-plus "Bliss" and "Crybaby") circle around the same melodic ideas to the point of tedium.

My *Rainbow* experience was further marred by prejudices I'd picked up in my preadolescence that I wouldn't shake until adulthood. In a matter of just a few years, I'd become embarrassed about loving Mariah. As a kid who sometimes went to nauseating lengths to act older and wiser than my age, I'd internalized the message that certain kinds of music deserved more attention than others — and that it wasn't worthwhile to take artists like Mariah seriously. I began gravitating to Fiona Apple, Sinéad O'Connor, and Tori Amos, confrontational singer-songwriters who had it in them to say "fuck you" to the world more belligerently than Mariah ever would. I was enamored with the neo-soul of Erykah Badu, who possessed a spiritual gravitas and curiosity that seemed, at least at the time, beyond Mariah's reach. With these new obsessions, I was staging a modest rebellion that existed entirely within my headphones. What could Mariah offer that would match this mood? Her carefree attitude didn't jibe with my increasingly urgent sense of music as a religion, a way of life.

I wanted emo Mariah, I guess, not class-clown Mariah. And since *Rainbow*'s most inspired moments are offered in a spirit of silly, giddy fun, it's taken me a long time to appreciate them. These days, I'm partial to "X-Girlfriend," a sassy mid-tempo that gave Mariah the chance to hook up again with the talented songwriter Kandi Burruss. Burruss was a member of the Jermaine Dupri–backed group Xscape, which was featured on the hip-hop remix of "Always Be My Baby," and she had a hand in composing two girl-group hits that same year: TLC's "No Scrubs" and Destiny's Child's "Bills Bills Bills." "X-Girlfriend" may seem minor alongside those classics, but it contains one of Mariah's cleverest performances, driven by a slack-jawed (but still highly rhythmic) mumble on the verses that handily indicates how unbothered she is by a romantic rival. Even better and wackier is "Did I Do That?," a sweet-and-sour mix of schoolyard taunt, smoothly multi-tracked vocals, and the whoops and hollers of New Orleans rappers Mystikal and Master P. Together, these two little-known tracks showcase Mariah's sense of humor, as well as her ongoing experimentation with less slick, more astringent sounds.

Still, there's a reason the question of seriousness looms over this juncture in Mariah's career, when the mood of self-conscious frivolity was thick. While it's true that many pop stars' legacies have been cemented with little more than naïve love songs and party anthems, the search for profundity persists, and remains inextricable from the experience of long-term fandom. The artists we let into our lives may not always be able to give us wisdom or transcendence, but now and then we seek assurance that something real is at stake—for them and for us. I'm not sure lambs would find Mariah's fun-loving side so prepossessing if we didn't know that there was something more complicated going on beneath the surface.

If Mariah had been content to be just any old pop star, maybe the idea of seriousness (or the lack thereof) wouldn't be so crucial. But the moment she started to show a surprising capacity for introspection, the press made a point of considering this very dilemma. A 1996 *Vibe* feature article pointed to her "seriously difficult time in the respect department. Critics acknowledge her technical prowess and her five-octave range, but they also dismiss her singing as trite and ostentatious, and her music as crossover fluff."[10] Such accusations would not have stung so much if something profound wasn't being overlooked.

On the early-internet message boards and listservs, where divadom could be dissected with partisan passion and energy, I found an early mentor on the matter: an older gentleman whom I would never meet in real life and whose name I can't remember. (Though I never knew his sexual orientation, I assumed even then that this was the first gay elder I'd ever encountered.) For what must have been a year, we exchanged messages about our favorite female singers, emails that today are buried in an inbox to which I have long since lost access. It was in those conversations that I first tried to articulate what these women meant to me, why they moved me, and how their voices comforted me.

For this man, the breeziness of *Rainbow* was not so easily dismissed. Did a woman have to always be pouring her heart out for us to consider her worth listening to? Couldn't this tone be read as Mariah's attempt at not letting the negativity in her life box her in? The album may not be a favorite of mine, but I fondly remember my pen pal's defense, and I'm sympathetic to it. At a time when it was hard to find an unreservedly positive appraisal of Mariah in any major publication, when even critical praise carried a hint of condescension, this stranger's assessment validated my desire to know that Mariah mattered. This desire, like my already obvious though still undeclared sexuality, was one for which I had only the most rudimentary language. In retrospect, I like to think my pen pal was teaching me, in his own indirect way, that escapism was key to any great diva's relationship with her queer fans — and that, ultimately, the fear of what's being escaped is never all that far from view.

Mariah's delight in what others might consider tacky, garish, or over-the-top went into high gear in the *Rainbow* era, and so did her queer appeal. Perhaps even more intentionally gay than the album's invocation of the rainbow — by then a widely recognized symbol of LGBTQ pride — is a theatrically stylized photo from this period, taken by LaChapelle for *Rolling Stone* in 2000, that depicts Mariah as a cheerleader who has stumbled into a men's locker room. Surrounded by a gaggle of half-naked dudes with rippling abs, she's at once the sexual object that heteronormative society would have these men covet and the gay icon whose presence throws their implied homoeroticism into relief. The image, a throwback to beefcake magazines of the '50s, suggests an almost conspiratorial affinity between Mariah and the gay lambs, who know that flamboyance, easily perceived as artificiality, is really a way of asserting that you don't give a damn about the haters and stiffs (in fact, it's the thing pop-diva excess and blinged-out rap machismo have in common). Through the lens of queerness, it's easy to see how Mariah's embrace of camp aesthetics, and her revelry in what others dismiss as unserious, allowed her to serve up defiance with a smile.

If Mariah's queer-friendly visual style comes across as more than a gimmick or put-on, it's because she understands that pleasure of any kind can be hard-won for people who are marginalized. She also knows that pleasure is no panacea. In her most confessional songs, there are no sweet nothings about *healing*, no false narratives of *closure*. For a gay person like me, who came into adulthood in the It-Gets-Better era of compulsory queer positivity, her ambivalence cuts deep, and her pessimism rings true. "You'll *always* be somewhere on the outside," goes one of her lines; "a part of me will *never* be quite able to feel stable," goes another.

In the age of Beyoncé, when diva femininity has become so tightly linked to ideas of self-empowerment, it's refreshing to remember how ill-suited Mariah is to the roles of girl boss and superwoman. (Even her well-documented struggles with her erratic voice, which she has partly attributed to nodules on her vocal cords, have a way of grounding her otherworldly talents in the reality of human imperfection.) The insecurities she sings about are distinctly her own — not a grab-bag of feelings engineered for maximum relatability. She's in no rush to assuage or overcome them, either. As she writes in her memoir, "Feelings are not like skin; there are no fresh new cells coming to replace ruined ones."[11]

Given those words, who can blame her for ensconcing herself among signifiers of prepubescent girlhood — the spray-paint rainbows and heart-shaped lollipops of her album art, the butterflies and petals of her song titles, the Hello Kitty accessories she's known to collect? If we're doomed to be forever haunted by the pains of youth, we may as well hold on to its pleasures too.

The diligent maintenance of good vibes can come at a cost. In accordance with the laws of pop entropy, everything began to fall apart.

Since the mid-1990s, Mariah had been wanting to try acting. Like many singers, she has a natural gift for mimicry: her impressions of Aretha Franklin, which she has whipped out on occasion in interviews, are spot-on, and her off-the-cuff jokes and comic timing suggest an ability to think and react on her feet, like a thespian. Acting lessons had become a form of therapeutic release toward the end of her marriage to Mottola, who had strongly discouraged her from pursuing the big screen. Newly divorced, Mariah was motivated to get her start.

The seeds of her first major film (initially titled *All That Glitters*) were planted in 1997, but her remaining obligations at Sony led to delays. "Heartbreaker," originally composed for the movie, instigated the completion of *Rainbow*, her final album of all-new material for the company. Screenwriter Kate Lanier was later hired to expand Mariah's story idea for the film, and, given her work on the Oscar-nominated Tina Turner biopic *What's Love Got to Do with It*, it seemed she'd be able to deliver a script that persuasively charts the rocky road to stardom. Renamed *Glitter*, the project was never intended to be strictly autobiographical, but its concept—a retooling of *A Star Is Born*, transposed to the early '8os—comes off as another effort to drive home the fact that Mariah's life was "*not* a fairy tale."

Behind the scenes, tribulations abounded. Mariah had fulfilled the terms of her Sony contract and landed at Virgin to the tune of $8o million, one of the biggest record deals ever. It was the label's artist-friendly reputation— built off the success of Lenny Kravitz (who had known Mariah since the two were struggling, unknown musicians in New York City) and a string of concept albums Janet Jackson released in the '9os—that attracted her. But the arrangement was another ring of hell. I remember Greil Marcus's observation that "what links the greatest rock 'n' roll careers is a volcanic ambition . . . in some cases, a refusal to know when to quit or even rest"[12] when I think of the already exhausted diva morphing into a late-capitalist zombie, permanently on call and dangerously sleep-deprived.

If there was anything that could replace the cheerful images that defined Mariah in the '9os, it was a public bloodletting. Moral concern about media coverage of celebrities had already become widespread with the death of Princess Diana in 1997, and things would only get worse in the years following the pilloried release of *Glitter* in 2001, as reporters and paparazzi flashed their fangs at Britney Spears and Lindsay Lohan. Mariah's career cataclysm may look minor in comparison, even forgettable. But certain episodes live on in the mind, not least of which is the prank she pulled at *Total Request Live*, a program of almost biblical significance to teen pop fans at the time. During the first stretch of promotion for *Glitter* and the soundtrack's lead single, "Loverboy," Mariah shimmied into MTV's Times Square studio pushing an ice-cream cart and performed a (quite innocent though later much tsk-tsked) striptease for the befuddled host, Carson Daly. Then, with that old, practiced smile on her face, she not so jokingly huffed, "Every now and then somebody needs a little therapy, and today is that moment for me."[13] It was a cry for help. But, again, the competing impulses of melancholia and levity opened the situation up to being misread; coming as part of a whimsical PR stunt, Mariah's depressive comment was met with ridicule instead of the compassion it deserved.

Given what Mariah later disclosed about this period of her life, her conduct on the show was, if anything, admirably controlled. Her memoir details a risky trip she took to Japan in the late '90s to beseech Sony Corporation chairman Norio Ohga to release her from Mottola's control—a story that illuminates how devalued and defenseless even the biggest pop stars can feel within a labyrinthine, multinational corporation in which music is merely one of several revenue streams. The book also alleges dirty dealings aimed at thwarting her post-Sony success: a sample of Yellow Magic Orchestra's "Firecracker" intended for

"Loverboy" mysteriously ended up in a hit record by Jennifer Lopez, one of Mottola's hottest priority artists, forcing Mariah to reconceive the track from scratch; promotional items for *Glitter* were seen snatched from record stores.

Even more harrowing was Mariah's relationship with her new label. In one section of her memoir, she describes being hunted down by her Virgin handlers and her own family as she tries to steal away for a few hours of shut-eye, first at a hotel and then at a couple of private residences. Each would-be haven proves permeable and unsafe. "Sleep," Mariah writes, "this basic human requirement, this simple comfort, became impossible to obtain."[14] The episode plays like an extended scene of hide-and-seek straight out of a paranoid thriller, and it ends with a Shakespearean betrayal by Mariah's mother, at the house the singer bought for her, handing her daughter over to the police with "an odd, knowing look, which felt like the equivalent of a secret-society handshake, some sort of white-woman-in-distress cop code."[15]

As much as the mafia-style ruthlessness of record companies is baked into pop legend, we're still not predisposed to thinking of celebrities as victims of the corporate machine, especially not those who have taken advantage of the system's once-deep pockets to secure the kind of longevity Mariah still enjoys. But wrapped up in the myth of all-American ambition is just another tale of exploitation, one that revolves around the grueling, around-the-clock work of artists who sometimes come from meager means and latch on to fame as their way out. It's tempting to project onto Mariah's retelling of her Y2K-era debacle the labor consciousness of someone ready to hit the picket lines (she's now known to mockingly refer to label executives as "the corporate morgue").[16] As she tells it, the specter of her economically insecure upbringing dogged her at every corner, pushing her to a breaking point: "I always felt the rug could be pulled out from under me."[17]

What to make of the long-gestating project around which all this dysfunction swirled? As though the back-stage chaos weren't enough of an obstacle, the *Glitter* soundtrack was released on September 11, 2001, cosmi-cally bad timing that threw the album against a backdrop of national tragedy and made the whole endeavor look shallow and disposable. The film trailed after it ten days later, tanking when it hit theaters. But for all the venom-ous ink that's been spilled over it (the *New York Times* called the movie "mostly dross, an unintentionally hilar-ious compendium of time-tested cinematic clichés"),[18] *Glitter* isn't a negligible artifact in the Mariah oeuvre, nor need it be understood as a fatally embarrassing one. Removed from the commercial expectations it failed to meet and the historical context into which it landed, the film can be appreciated as a document of how one of the world's greatest pop stars saw herself at the time, and how she hoped to be seen.

Like many of its showbiz-drama antecedents, *Glitter* softens its study of the cold-blooded entertainment indus-try by framing it within a conventional love story. The romance here is between young, up-and-coming singer Billie Frank (played by Mariah) and a DJ named Julian "Dice" Black (Max Beesley), who becomes her creative collaborator and a driving force behind her career. By turns beneficent and abusive, professional and personal, their relationship reflects some of the ambivalent feel-ings Mariah has expressed about Mottola, whose guidance made her worldwide fame possible but whose oppressive rule left lasting scars. Ultimately, Billie and Dice's dynamic becomes so riven by his jealousy and paranoia that only his death can make him remotely sympathetic again, a last-minute twist that allows the film to close out with an obligatory ballad in his honor. But even with the obvious parallels to Mottola, there isn't much new to glean about Mariah from this part of the story. The scenes depicting the two lovers are so flat and lugubrious, our attention ends up drifting elsewhere.

Much more compelling is the R&B lineage the movie maps from the outset. Mariah and Lanier flip the racial makeup of the singer's parentage so that Billie's mother is a Black woman, a down-and-out lounge singer abandoned by a barely identified middle-class white man. Apart from ensuring that the film won't be read as a straightforward autobiography, this inversion encourages us to infer that the heroine's soulful singing style is a genetic inheritance, rather than a skill acquired through study or osmosis. For a mixed-race woman like Mariah, whose relationship to Black music had been scrutinized at various points throughout her career, reconfiguring her family background in this way seems to have offered her a chance to imagine a scenario in which those authenticity debates could be rendered moot.

In the opening scene, we get the first of several moments in which Billie's vocals are presented as a big reveal, a beacon from out of the blue. Billie's mother, intoxicated, invites her young daughter onto the nightclub stage, and together they riff up a storm on a song about not being able to turn a lover loose. The child's voice, passionate and pliable, is thrown down like a gauntlet. The scene dramatizes a kind of affirmation Mariah had long craved: recognition not just of her talent but of her identity.

After Billie is separated from her mother and thrown into the foster-care system, the film quickly flashes forward, and the classic soul of the parent–child duet is contrasted with the heavily synthesized R&B of the early '80s. We're introduced to the Manhattan demimonde young-adult Billie inhabits as she ascends to fame: a world of packed clubs, zany outfits, shiftless scenesters, and industry phonies, scored by a soundtrack of R&B gems such as D Train's "You're the One for Me" and Zapp's "Dance Floor." If nothing else, *Glitter* is a welcome opportunity to contemplate how much Black pop changed within just a few decades, a historical perspective almost entirely absent from Hollywood movies. Later in the film, we're treated to yet another variation of R&B when Billie buys her lover a Yamaha DX7, the quintessential '80s synth. The moment occasions a vision of Mariah as a singer-songwriter at the keys, à la Roberta Flack, composing introspective ballads. These period details allow us to consider Mariah in relation to various tributaries of Black music's past.

It's this attentiveness to R&B as a multifaceted tradition, the product of an ever-evolving history, that makes the *Glitter* soundtrack an intriguing listen, one that has never gotten its critical due. To help her with the album, Mariah brought in super-producer duo Jimmy Jam and Terry Lewis, who had worked with her on *Rainbow* and whose funky, electronic Minneapolis aesthetic dominated the '80s. Throughout their collaboration, you can hear the joy of Mariah the fan. Several moments on the album are exercises in fidelity. Jam and Lewis's original instrumental for Cherrelle's "I Didn't Mean to Turn You On" provides the foundation for Mariah's own cover, a recurring up-tempo theme in the film. And one of the inexplicably under-promoted selling points of the soundtrack is a previously unreleased original composition by Rick James, "All My Life," a seduction number worthy of Vanity 6 and the Mary Jane Girls. Amid these period references, Mariah's singing is fresh and audacious, as on the ballad "Lead the Way," in which her elaborate riffs are spiced up with unexpected, bluesy chromatic notes that reveal the growing sophistication of her musical ear.

Mariah had never attempted such a sustained tribute to a bygone period of Black culture, and her love of this era is palpable in the ease with which she recreates its signature styles. But the choice of the '80s was a brave one. She couldn't have been sure that the decade was far enough in the past to inspire collective nostalgia. And, at the turn of the millennium, R&B revivalism was invested in another decade — the '70s — whose upliftment politics and acoustic sounds inspired neo-soul artists accustomed to a lot more critical respect than Mariah ever received. Unlike them, Mariah was exploring a pulpier, less reputable chapter in the genre's history, one that was burdened by a glut of one- and two-hit wonders and a lingering bias against electronic instrumentation.

As with most retro-pastiche projects by contemporary artists, there's an ersatz aspect to the whole affair, a risk of glorified karaoke. But the results are consistently vibrant. Listening to Mariah's marvelous seven-minute take on the Indeep classic "Last Night a DJ Saved My Life," you have no trouble imagining her as queen of the discotheque; the lyrics, which describe a heartbroken clubber's grateful surrender to a groove, encapsulate Mariah's own oft-repeated claims that music rescued her from a tragic fate. In her hands, a dance-floor anthem takes on confessional dimensions. Threatening to disrupt the album's throwback vibe are a host of contemporary rappers, including Ja Rule, Fabolous, and Mystikal, who seem teleported in from the future. These helpings of early-2000s hip-hop are not only seamlessly integrated, they also serve as another stop on the soundtrack's journey across Black music's space-time continuum.

Mariah has been so haunted by the critical and commercial disaster of *Glitter* that for years she couldn't even utter the word. But just as it became a punch line, that same word also signified a doubling down on the gay aesthetics she had embraced in the *Rainbow* era. Scholar Nicole Seymour notes in her study on the cultural resonances of (and backlash against) glitter that the shiny substance — a fixture of drag shows, pride parades, and LGBTQ activist events — has long been associated with "identities and subject positions [that] have been devalued, ridiculed, and treated as unpolitical or unimportant in mainstream Western cultures."[19] That Mariah decided to name her big-screen debut — a film that so obviously draws inspiration from her own life — after this symbol of artifice, excess, marginality, and non-respectability shows us something she shares with many of her queer fans: her pain is forever bound up with the performative strategies with which she's learned to transmute it.

When I think of this period in Mariah's career, what comes to mind even before the media circus or the underrated *Glitter* soundtrack is her onscreen performance. Her acting in this film may be clumsy — it certainly lacks the quiet sensitivity she would bring to her scrupulously unglamorous supporting role as a social worker in Lee Daniels's 2009 film *Precious* — but there's an honesty that cuts through: a timidity reminiscent of her downcast, childlike gaze in that 1999 *Oprah* interview, and a sort of squirmy stage fright we don't tend to associate with otherwise ostentatious divas.

Throughout the movie, Mariah falls back on two recurring expressions: a high-beam grin that veils Billie's incurable sadness, and a cringe that verges on tears. You look at her in certain scenes and you see a woman who has had to wear a smile for so long that she's forgotten how to relax her facial muscles. She looks perpetually indecisive; the dueling demands of melancholia and levity are etched into her face. Her stiff, clenched disposition — what the *Village Voice* critic Michael Atkinson described as the look of someone who's "lost her car keys"[20] — has a poignancy that's unique to nonprofessional and inexperienced actors. It's a quality that can't be faked; after all, you don't *learn* how to be an amateur. Mariah's unsteadiness as an actor stands in contrast with her vocal genius, which the film figures as innate, untaught, reliably present since youth. There's a tenderness that comes with such a public display of inadequacy, and there's something sobering about seeing a virtuoso like Mariah thrown out of her league.

If the late 1990s and early 2000s found Mariah caught between raw emotion and surface-level vivacity, then her awkward performance in *Glitter* was one of her most eloquent enactments of that tug-of-war. Every time I watch the film, I'm reminded of James Baldwin's famous insight about movie stars: "One does not go to see them act: one goes to watch them *be*."[21] It's through that magnanimously curious view of onscreen behavior that we can open ourselves to the fallibility that makes our overachieving diva human. There's beauty in a blunder, a stammer, a false start. *Glitter* doesn't have to be salvageable as a work of cinematic art to contain something fans can cherish. Here and there, sometimes against its own intentions, *Glitter* makes visible the same quivering vulnerability that fuels Mariah's most personal music.

# 6

# BACK AT NUMBER 1

How and when we're introduced to an artist's body of work shapes our expectations of it, and long careers offer an array of entry points. For me, Mariah Carey's R&B renaissance in the mid-1990s is as central an emblem of my youth as any memory I can call forth, musical or otherwise. This is the version of her I think of most readily. But that period was not her only golden age, and the more I encounter fans who are older or younger than me, the more I wonder what it would have been like to fall in love with her from another generational vantage. For many fans still in their twenties as of this writing (including the R&B singers Ella Mai, Normani, Kehlani, and Summer Walker, who have spoken about being inspired by Mariah), the commercial resurgence that accompanied 2005's *The Emancipation of Mimi* seems to be the definitive moment, the one around which the past and present orbit.

Younger fans are more likely to have discovered Mariah at a time when her R&B and hip-hop bona fides were no longer the subject of constant debate. They heard her within a landscape that had long since been transformed by her genre-blending influence, and came to know her as a vital participant in that crowded field, not as an elder put out to pasture. Too young to remember how omnipresent Mariah had once been, they may not have understood how precipitously she had fallen, or how important her revival was to those who had followed her since the beginning. They didn't know, as I did, what it meant to yearn for this great diva's return to glory, and to fear that it might never happen. They weren't stuck in a habit of weighing every new record against the various forms of baggage she was carrying.

Partly because of such baggage, comebacks can be genuinely moving to witness. But there can be something artificial about them too. When a star is no longer the hottest name on the scene, her against-all-odds defiance of time and decay becomes low-hanging PR fruit. If this tradition didn't exist, record companies would have had to invent it. The spectacle of vindication serves to assure us that what the industry produces isn't all disposable, that certain talents are eternal. Comebacks are useful not just in extending a career into the future but in keeping the idea of a back catalog relevant and monetizable.

Though they may seem like a showbiz commonplace, rebirths on the scale of Mariah's *Emancipation* era are rare. Part of the reason is that only a handful of artists have occupied her elite realm of long-term global fame. Elvis Presley's mid-career revival in 1968 comes to mind as an example of a comparably gargantuan act so gloriously and unexpectedly recapturing their luster after years of public indifference. Most superstars are not so lucky; even Michael Jackson was forced to chase the high of *Thriller* until the end of his days, staging ever more colossal displays of ambition to diminishing returns. All pop artists are eventually forced to realize that new trends will supplant what came before, pressuring them to adapt their style at the risk of vexing a core fanbase that seeks the comfort of the familiar. Under these conditions, even the flimsiest pop song can become a profound symbol, an embodiment of time's passage. The threat of obsolescence is what augments music's allure as it marches from the top-forty chart to the oldies station. Through a pop star's aging, we experience our own.

A lot happened in the four years between *Glitter* and *The Emancipation of Mimi*, but none of it made Mariah's comeback inevitable. Her historic contract with Virgin was bought out for $28 million, severing her ties with a label that showed no inclination to come to her rescue. She then signed a deal with Island Records, where executive Lyor Cohen (who had overseen the careers of some of the greatest rap acts of the 1980s and '90s, including Slick Rick, EPMD, and De La Soul) took an interest in rehabilitating her reputation.

Though met with lukewarm sales and mostly unsympathetic reviews, 2002's *Charmbracelet* is an excellent transitional record, distinguished by some of Mariah's liveliest songwriting in years. Aside from the lachrymose lead single, "Through the Rain" (a sort of "Hero" retread, meant to commemorate her triumph over the *Glitter* adversity), and the downbeat "I Only Wanted" (whose Spanish guitar recalls "My All"), it's light on adult-contemporary fare. The dearth of pop-diva ballads signaled that Mariah wasn't all that desperate to woo back her middle-of-the-road fans, regardless of the consequences of neglecting them. Mariah's coproducers on *Charmbracelet* all hail from the worlds of R&B and hip-hop, and their sinuous soundscapes create the perfect setting for some of the most rap-like singing she'd ever recorded, extending the innovations of *Butterfly*.

On the Jermaine Dupri collaboration "The One," she serves up seething romantic anxiety on a bed of lace, rapid-fire lines tumbling out of her mouth in a cool, vaporous tone. Another rhythmically tricky gem is "Clown," a track by the Philadelphia duo Dre & Vidal, who had come to prominence a couple years earlier with their work for neo-soul stars Jill Scott and Musiq Soulchild. The song is one of Mariah's iciest kiss-offs, and it marks the first time she'd engaged in anything like a hip-hop beef. Rumor has it that the target of the lyrics is Eminem, who'd bragged to the press about the two having dated, prompting Mariah's unbothered denials ("you should have never intimated we were lovers / when you know very well we never even touched each other"). Neither song is widely known, but both highlight her ever-sharpening facility at fusing her own lush melodic sensibilities with contemporary hip-hop's jittery cadences.

Contrasting with the electronically driven aesthetic of these tracks are a few instances of acoustic instrumentation. "Subtle Invitation" features a vibrant horn section, and "Sunflowers for Alfred Roy"—an understated tribute to Mariah's father, with whom she shared a cathartic exchange before his death from cancer in 2002—builds to a minor-key bridge awash in stormy strings. In the latter, Mariah doesn't try to compete with the swelling arrangement behind her; the final verse exposes her voice briefly cracking from heartbreak, a rare glimpse of imperfection from a singer known to tinker obsessively with her studio vocals.

Despite several outstanding tracks, nothing about *Charmbracelet* feels like a go-for-broke bid for career resuscitation. For much of the album, Mariah sounds so indifferent to the pressures of delivering a surefire pop hit that you imagine she may have been secretly happy to be in a commercial slump: perhaps less scrutiny would grant her freedom to write and sing however she pleased. The breathiness of her performances accentuates this relaxed mood. Though singers know that whispering creates considerable tension on the vocal cords — Mariah has called the effect a "fragile"[1] one — that strenuousness isn't what comes across to listeners. Whispering and suspirating, the diva sounds much more laid-back than when she's crying out in full voice.

Breathiness had been an important element in Mariah's music since the beginning (listen, for example, to the long, open-vowel exhalations in the minute-long outro of "Till the End of Time," from 1991). As a vocal arranger, she often required it of her background singers; Kelly Price has said that when recording with Mariah, she was taught "to lock into other textures of my voice — airier textures, lighter textures," qualities that diverged from the gut-punching gospel attack Price had learned from her COGIC upbringing: "We'd be in the vocal booth and she'd say, 'Put an H at the beginning of that word.'"[2] When Mariah was crowned the greatest singer of the MTV era in a program that ran on the channel in 2005, rapper Fat Joe also stressed this aspect of her sound: the "cloudy voice that just puts you in a dream world."[3]

In the past, Mariah usually offered her breathy tones as a kind of musical amuse-bouche, tiding the listener over until the belting could commence. But on *Charmbracelet*, air is as much the main attraction as the singer's earth-shaking belts. There's a lot that can be read into this vocal affectation. A whisper draws us into the realm of the erotic. It calls to mind the softness and wetness of the oral cavity, a secret purred into a lover's ear, the accelerated respiration of climax (one might think of Diana Ross's heavy sighs on "Love Hangover" and Donna Summer's moans on "Love to Love You Baby" as precursors). On *Charmbracelet*'s second single, "Boy (I Need You)," Mariah's whisper is coy and Marilyn Monroe–like; every note dissolves in our ears upon contact, like cotton candy on the tongue. Elsewhere, the sound proves to be more than a tool of sexual enticement. On "Clown," it's abrasive, hissing, thick with contempt. On "Through the Rain," it evokes the vulnerability of a frightened child soothing herself to sleep.

Years later, Mariah would say in an interview, "I don't like to belt all the time—it's boring as hell."[4] Her prioritization of breathiness in the *Charmbracelet* era allowed her to pivot away from music built single-mindedly around climaxes, toward forms of expression that evoke ephemerality, eschew neat resolutions, and invite fans to listen with heightened attention. Mariah's whisper rivals any other part of her voice, and with its subtle gradations it is capable of a multitude of emotional effects. In the history of vocal performance, this style can also be heard as a mark of modernity. Only with advanced recording technology can we reliably capture these diaphanous tones, which would have been inaudible in the unmiked saloons and concert halls of the past.

No one would call Mariah's voice small, but when she's singing on the edge of the air, I think of her in the tradition of great sighers, from Shirley Horn to Helen Merrill. But what a sigh can't really convey is strength, power, dominion—qualities on which most pop comebacks are predicated. In recent R&B, which tends to lean on this dreamy, narcotized sound, the sigh has become even more of a flash point than it was when Mariah first helped popularize it. In 2020, the soul belter K. Michelle attacked whispery-voiced singers as "people who got balls in their mouths, who don't even open their mouths," whose music is "like one big, long lullaby."[5] Her assessment conveys a certain old-school soul ethic, in which authentic R&B vocal style hinges on the forceful and dramatic declaration of one's emotions, not wimpy capitulation to them.

Perhaps to reestablish Mariah's diva primacy, *Charmbracelet*'s follow-up took a different tack. *The Emancipation of Mimi* is a flex of traditional singerly prowess, a return to marathon belting reminiscent of the vocal exhibition-ism of her early years. While working on the album, Dupri urged Mariah to get back to what he called "straight singing": "Her full voice, that's what people fell in love with, and that's what I wanted to make sure was different with these songs."[6] If there's one thing I remember most about first hearing *Emancipation* in 2005, it's the feeling that I hadn't heard Mariah wail so passionately, track after track, since the '90s. The album set my ears ringing. And what could signal freedom better than one of the world's greatest singers taking up the maximum amount of sonic space?

During the press tour for *The Emancipation of Mimi*, Mariah characterized the album as a party record: "With *Charmbracelet* everyone wanted to hear the stories of my trials and tribulations . . . Now I'm like, okay, we've done that, this record is about having some fun."[7] Forgive me, then, if I linger here on the high caliber of the ballads. Extending the acoustic vibes of "Subtle Invitation," several of the best songs here are slow burners decked out with brassy, sepia-toned instrumentation, amid which Mariah's voice is prominently placed.

For the first time, Mariah worked with James Poyser, a brilliant songwriter associated with the musical collective Soulquarians, who were responsible for the hot-buttered magic of such neo-soul landmarks as Erykah Badu's *Mama's Gun* and D'Angelo's *Voodoo*. Poyser's contribution, "Mine Again," is a thunderclap of a torch song. Starting with the vinyl crackle in its opening seconds, it's a faithful homage to soul music at its most fervid and intense, calling to mind a bygone era of belters who weren't afraid to beg for love until their throats went hoarse.

A plea for the return of an old flame, "Mine Again" is centered on a blazingly resonant D5 note that, enveloped by horns, is itself like a wind instrument blasted at deafening volume. In the final stretch of the song, that power note is pushed — perilously — a half-step higher. If Mariah's best singing in the '90s was characterized by an illusion of complete freedom, here her instrument, poignantly weathered by age and use, seems to sense its own ceiling. This is crucial to the impact of the performance. Vocal strain is a key ingredient in a lot of classic soul; many of the great singers of the genre deploy it as a mark of realness, striving toward some elusive beyond, projecting past boundaries of decorum to access the "deep hurt" Amiri Baraka described as native to the music. I'm thinking not just of virtuoso belters in the league of Aretha Franklin and Patti LaBelle but of singers less technically polished: Otis Redding, whose highest notes often sound like they've been squeezed out of his body at great cost, or Lorraine Ellison, whose belting devolves into a series of primal screams at the end of her signature hit, "Stay with

Me Baby." These are performers who know how to use the gnarly extremes of the voice to build drama and emotional suspense.

The key change in the last chorus of "Mine Again" wouldn't have its galvanic force if we didn't have some trepidation that Mariah's voice might not reach its target (and if she hadn't decided to render her inhalations so audible in the opening verse, prompting us to imagine her preparing to expel every ounce of energy from her diaphragm). An exclamatory "maybe" at the end of the song is so guttural, it lands in our ears like a splat, giving us the feeling that the diva has only barely made it out in one piece.

By the mid-2000s, R&B was emerging from a stretch of years in which brash, twitchy electronic beats had dominated the scene, thanks to futuristic-minded producers such as Timbaland and Rodney Jerkins. But neo-soul's success had brought warmer, brighter sounds back into rotation, moving them from the margins of pop into the mainstream again, revealing a nostalgia well-suited to the turning of a millennium. Mariah mines this retro inclination throughout *Emancipation*. "Mine Again" finds a companion soul-wrencher in "Circles," cowritten by "Big Jim" Wright, a former member of the gospel group Sounds of Blackness who would go on to become Mariah's music director. The not-yet-requited-love ballad "I Wish You Knew" features a spoken verse reminiscent of Diana Ross's "Ain't No Mountain High Enough" and the Chi-Lites' "Have You Seen Her." And on "Stay the Night," a hip-hop beat strikes up a dialogue with classic R&B and jazz via a sample of Ramsey Lewis's "Betcha by Golly, Wow," a piano rendition of the Stylistics' Philly soul classic.

These nods to the past live comfortably alongside the

album's contemporary-sounding tracks, several of which bear Dupri's signature. During the recording of *Emancipation*, L. A. Reid, the newly installed chairman of Island Records, encouraged Mariah to link up with her old friend in Atlanta, believing the two could rekindle some of the magic they'd achieved on "Always Be My Baby" and deliver another hit. Big ballads weren't on the agenda when the pair first teamed up for the project. In their early sessions, Mariah and Dupri focused on club-friendly fare, including "Shake It Off," a delectable mix of speed-singing and punchy doo-wop embellishments laid atop a beeping pulse. Originally earmarked as the album's lead single (and eventually released as its third), the song further refines what had long since become Mariah's wheelhouse. Tightly coiled and tantalizingly rhythmic, her vocals prance across the beat with the precision of an acrobat's movements.

On this and another Dupri contribution, "It's Like That," Mariah's lyrics emphasize her knack for tongue-in-cheek product placement (Calgon, Bacardi, and Louis Vuitton are among the brands mentioned) and blithe shade-throwing. The latter song aims one of her most ingenious witticisms—"Them chickens is ash and I'm lotion"—at anyone who might try to kill her "hot tamale" vibe. Elsewhere on the album, this exuberance is applied to scenes of seduction: in Dupri's "Get Your Number" and the percussion-drenched Neptunes tracks "Say Somethin'" and "To the Floor," the singer is caught up in an erotic intrigue with a suitor who might turn out to be bad news. Mariah wasn't romantically linked to anyone at the time, and from these songs you get the sense of a self-possessed woman on the prowl, thirsty for love but wise to the rituals of attraction. Repeatedly, she lays down terms for the man in her midst while also assuring him she's open to what the night will bring.

In these tracks, you hear the fun-loving, celebratory spirit Mariah was touting in interviews. But it was heartbreak that won out on the charts. "We Belong Together" — a Dupri track that would plant Mariah at the top of the Hot 100 for fourteen weeks, the longest time any hit of the 2000s spent in that coveted slot — reconciles the album's twin impulses, setting unshakable angst against a programmed kick-drum and hi-hat pattern as window-rattling as the singer's voice. Mariah had been releasing songs in this mold since 1997's "Breakdown," but none of them had gone to the top of the pop charts. The massive success of "We Belong Together" was pivotal in transforming what casual listeners thought a Mariah ballad could sound like.

As Dupri tells it, Mariah "was pushing for something more ghetto," and he had to maneuver the track toward a poppier middle. "We finally agreed on what she called 'a thugged-out ballad,'"[8] he writes in his memoir. A precursor for the track can be found on the album that had brought Dupri career-defining success a year earlier: Usher's *Confessions*, which sold eight million units, a rare feat in the post-Napster era. *Confessions*' biggest ballad, "Burn," found Dupri hammering down a winning formula, striking a balance between unrelenting rhythmic propulsion, heartfelt vocals, and spiraling melodic lines — hooks that sometimes sound like digressions. It's a testament to how inspired he and his two songwriting partners, Johntá Austin and Manuel Seal, were in this peak moment of new-millennium R&B that "We Belong Together" is less a variation on the "Burn" blueprint than the apotheosis of a modern kind of sad love song. And it's a sign of Mariah's authority as a behind-the-scenes collaborator that the track, from its zigzagging, conversational lyrics to its delicately multitracked ad-libs, ends up sounding like nothing less than incontrovertibly hers.

The juxtaposition of old-fashioned song craft and hip-hop swagger comes right at the top, with a tinkling keyboard quickly followed by some brief, airy vocalizing and then a loud, thudding beat. The bulk of the song is performed in an even-keeled middle register—no startling lows or highs just yet, no swinging for the fences. The notes are crowded together without much melodic or temporal distance between them, lending a claustrophobic quality to the verses. Mariah snakes her way through the beat, first listlessly, then swiftly, in dense syllabic clusters that bring a feeling of acceleration at varying intervals. Aside from clever allusions to Bobby Womack's "If You Think You're Lonely Now" and The Deele's '80s quiet-storm hit "Two Occasions" (the latter written by Mariah's former collaborator Babyface), the lyrics are fairly formulaic: the heroine is hung up on her ex; she can't get over him, and he couldn't care less.

What sets the song apart is the almost unbearable degree of tension it achieves through minute shifts of rhythm and cadence. Boxed into her mid-range, Mariah finds a kind of mobility in the rapid clip of her lyrics, and as the verbiage gets even more tongue-twisty in the second verse, we marvel at how the destabilizing power of lost love could have granted the singer such pinpoint articulation. We wonder when she'll be able to catch her breath. Then, just as things start winding down, Mariah knocks the chorus up an octave, a rupture in the song's fabric made even more unnerving by the fact that Dupri's beat keeps carrying on, relentless and indifferent to the singer's pain. If that man she's singing to was content to ignore her cries for the first three-quarters of the track, now there can be no doubt that he can at least hear them. The high notes—withheld until the last possible moment and sung with unfussy purposefulness—are an index of love's ability to shock and derange its victim.

In his book *Love Songs: The Hidden History*, Ted Gioia writes about the shame that attaches to pop expressions of romantic devotion: "Even those who listen to love songs and know the words *by heart* (and who doesn't) adopt a public posture that this is *wimpy* music, for emotional weaklings and sentimental fools."[9] For years, I'd downplayed my Mariah fandom for this reason; as far back as the *Rainbow* era, I'd been suspicious of my love for her, keeping it mostly to myself.

Some of this was youthful self-righteousness. Adolescence awakens us to the chaos and injustice of the world, and mine was shaped by the start of the Iraq War and the fight for LGBTQ rights. However half-heartedly, I was sympathetic to the belief that pathetic love songs were self-absorbed, almost immoral—and that to be enticed by visions of heteronormative codependency was to be swindled. By my teenage years, I was trying to distance myself from a few homophobic people in my life, and anything that didn't align with that goal—anything that made torturous attachments sound exquisite—seemed like a betrayal of the emancipated self I hoped to become.

But, despite my loftiest ideals, I could never really deny my weakness for ballads. I'd grown up with them: the towering divas of Cantonese and Mandarin pop — Teresa Teng, Paula Tsui, Anita Mui, Priscilla Chan — had preceded Mariah as my childhood idols, and they all sang with the same unapologetic weepiness as she did. The feeling that these ballads gave me was the closest thing to romance I'd ever experienced. And by the time "We Belong Together" was released, I certainly didn't need my elder gay pen pal to explain their power to me. I knew how it felt to fall for someone and get my heart broken, to stash my desires away in the gloom of a closet. I'd become a pro at that, and here Mariah was, reminding me that she was one too. I needed her monuments to unrequited love like I hadn't before.

Because the song was playing everywhere in 2005 — all across my college campus, as well as in Beijing, where I studied abroad that summer — it seemed as if almost everyone I knew was being drawn into fellowship with her voice and the torment I heard in it. You couldn't avoid this song if you tried; its incessant presence on the radio mimicked the exhausting, repetitious cycles of an infatuation that refuses to loosen its grip. And so, regardless of our musical preferences, we were all forced to pay collective attention to an artist who had seemed like a pop relic just a few months ago, but who was now one of our preeminent chroniclers of amour fou, reflecting the tangle of our not-so-grown-up emotions back to us.

The sweet agony in "We Belong Together" — captured again in the irresistible companion pieces "Don't Forget About Us" from 2005 and "I Stay in Love" from 2008, both cowritten by Mariah, Dupri, and his associates — would continue to serve as an emotional anchor for a star persona that was both vivacious and aloof. Where the *Rainbow* and *Charmbracelet* eras found Mariah rocking jeans and tank tops, the *Emancipation* media blitz often pictured her dressed in expensive gowns, a look meant to emphasize her empress-like indomitability. She was seen hobnobbing with fashion bigwigs such as André Leon Talley and Donatella Versace, and a few years later satirized her own glamour-puss style in an MTV commercial that depicted her play-exercising on a treadmill in stiletto heels. The shiny gold garment she's wearing on the *Emancipation* album cover "is not even a dress," she told *Billboard*. "It's something that wraps around your body. It's so weird, but you just had to be confident in wearing something like that . . . I was just in a moment where it's like, 'Look, people may have written me off, but I will never write myself off.'"[10]

As a fan who had grown to care about Mariah (even in the moments when I was trying to reject her), I relished everything about her comeback. Her music was as confident as ever, and she also looked happy and in control of her life. For the first time she seemed to enjoy being pampered. Wealth had already become part of her brand; a famous episode of *MTV Cribs* from 2002 showed off her Tribeca penthouse and its butterfly wallpaper, cavernous closets, and cutesy pink decor. Even when such opulence struck me as cartoonishly grotesque, I couldn't help but enjoy the winking, camped-up irony with which she flaunted her luxurious lifestyle (a simulacrum of the old-Hollywood glamour she'd loved as a child) and the goofily imperious way she drawled that great staple of her vocabulary: "dahhling."

*Emancipation*'s follow-up, $E=MC^2$, prolonged the triumph. Its biggest hit, "Touch My Body," helped her surpass Elvis Presley as the solo artist with the most Number 1 hits on the Hot 100. Impeccably written and produced, the album is stacked with potential hit records, made in collaboration with young talents such as Danja, The-Dream, and Scott Storch. Amid these producers' up-to-the-minute flourishes, Mariah is effervescent and catchy, even if at times a bit impersonal. The opening track, "Migrate," is one of her funniest. Narrating a girls' night out in hilariously granular detail, the song is also something of a sonic joke. It begins with a staccato riff sung in Mariah's whistle register and ends with auto-tuned vocals from the rapper T-Pain, a clever juxtaposition that invites us to consider all the bizarre and surreal guises that the human voice has adopted over the course of pop history.

As current as $E=MC^2$ sounded in 2008, it's clear that legacy was weighing on Mariah's mind. The bridge of "For the Record," another highlight, weaves together titles of some of her own favorite songs, challenging fans to catch each reference. She'd always been an allusive artist, but in moments like this, the reference is herself and the breadth of her own oeuvre. This retrospective frame of mind prompts us to reflect on how far Mariah had come since her debut as a soft-spoken singer-songwriter with a booming voice almost two decades earlier. Her music had changed a lot since then, and so had the surrounding pop landscape. The adult-contemporary ballads that had once been her bread and butter were all but absent from the charts now, and little did anyone know that R&B's commercial golden age was approaching its end. In fact, *The Emancipation of Mimi* is the last full-fledged R&B record by a Black artist to be the top-selling album of its year.

Coherence is hardly a requirement for pop legacies, but it can help imbue a fan's decades-long investment with a sense of meaning. What makes Mariah's body of work come together as a unified whole, despite its stylistic twists and turns? One of my favorite moments from this era attempts to answer that question, to reconcile Mariah's past with her present. At a brief promotional concert for *Emancipation* on BET, she chose to perform "Vision of Love." Her debut single was something of a genre chameleon, embraced by R&B-loving audiences but often perceived as an adult-contemporary ballad. When the song won a Grammy Award in 1991, it was slotted in the pop category. In revisiting it alongside a set of new, distinctly urban material, Mariah was reasserting its roots in Black music. And just as she had performed "Vision of Love" at Harlem's legendary Apollo Theater at the time of its release, she was singing it now before a predominantly Black crowd. That same month, the importance of this detail was driven home by a cover profile in *Essence* magazine that proclaimed her "America's Most Misunderstood Black Woman" — an echo of a 1991 *Ebony* article headlined "Not Another White Girl Trying to Sing Black."

Mariah's voice had changed since the '90s, with a new, not-unpleasant squeakiness in its timbre. But her slightly diminished vocal power doesn't prevent this performance from being one of the most fiery and daringly improvisational she has ever delivered — a necessary reminder, in an age when studio vocals are polished to within an inch of their lives, of just how much her music owes to raw, stand-and-deliver mastery. Wails, growls, bellows, whistles, whispers, and lightning-speed runs: over the course of four spellbinding minutes, she holds nothing back from her arsenal. On the line "Prayed through the nights / *so* faithfully," she lets out a fearsome lion's roar, powered by the kind of white-knuckle conviction experience can bestow. Even if the concept of the comeback strikes you as an industry contrivance, the intensity of her singing on that stage might convince you that Mariah's, at least, was the real deal. In the context of everything we knew about her struggles in the early 2000s, "Vision of Love" registers here, for the first time, as a testimony. She'd written it as a teenager, and now she was inviting us to interpret her life as the manifestation of the song's message.

# 7

# A TIMELESS DIVA THROUGH TIME

Since the beginning of the 2010s, Mariah Carey has released only three studio albums, a notable decrease in productivity from an artist who made seven in her first decade and five in her second. During this period, her personal life has kept her busy: she was married to actor and TV personality Nick Cannon for eight years and gave birth to twins in 2011. At times, she appears to have settled happily into legacy mode, relying on her Christmas music to keep her name a permanent fixture of the holidays. Even as this yuletide strategy risks turning her into a caricature of herself, forever reselling the same repertoire in ever shinier packaging, it's proven incredibly savvy. Thanks to Mariah's tireless promotion, numerous cover versions, and its use as a plot device in the popular 2003 romantic comedy *Love Actually*, "All I Want for Christmas Is You" has become no less a global standard than "Happy Birthday." Beginning in 2019, it has shot to Number 1 on pop charts around the world every December.

The fact that so much of Mariah's long-term fame has been secured with a single song she wrote in 1994 — a song that intentionally evokes a cozy idyll of an earlier era — underscores how much her catalog has become an object of nostalgia. The lengthy waits between albums have further heightened the retrospective quality of Mariah fandom. These days, the adoration Mariah receives from the lambs is tinged with protectiveness, fueled by the idea that her achievements are in need not just of praise but of vociferous defense. Given that she remains one of the most successful pop stars of all time, what accounts for this anxiety? By sticking up for our beloved diva, are we trying to protect something from our childhoods—something that feels even more precious for having been, at times, as uncool as we ourselves may have once been?

In some ways, this urge to see Mariah validated as more than a commercial juggernaut is starting to feel obsolete. Over the past few decades, the tides have turned in pop's favor, and the early-2000s ascendance of "poptimism"— an ideology that has sought to undermine the critical establishment's preference for white male-led rock and direct attention to musicians working in less vaunted genres—has resulted in the reappraisal of artists like her. Nineties R&B is now regarded as a venerable style whose influence has seeped into unexpected places (for example, the adventurous indie-pop singer Grimes has said that Mariah's voice "shattered the fabric of my existence,"[1] and the lo-fi rockers Sufjan Stevens, Rosie Thomas, and the Shins have unironically covered "Always Be My Baby"). In 2022, the staff of *Pitchfork*, a millennial arbiter of all that is important in rock music, did something that would have been unthinkable when the publication launched in 1996, right in the middle of the *Daydream* era: they named the Bad Boy remix of "Fantasy" the greatest song of the '90s.

It can no longer be said that Mariah has never been talked about as an architect of contemporary pop. But for some fans, memories of anti-Mariah sentiment still sting. In 1996, *Daydream* was up for six Grammy Awards and was favored by some prognosticators to win but was ultimately shut out of every category—Album of the Year went to Alanis Morissette's *Jagged Little Pill*, a paragon of the kind of singer-songwriter confessionalism typically honored by Grammy voters. Veteran music journalist and former *Vibe* editor-in-chief Danyel Smith recalls the results of the evening as an intentional slight—"a shaming."[2] One of countless examples of white rockers being favored over Black R&B and hip-hop artists at the Grammy Awards, the incident was partially echoed in 2006, when *The Emancipation of Mimi* nabbed a few non-televised trophies but lost the most coveted honor to U2's *How to Dismantle an Atomic Bomb*.

Lamenting industry snubs that most music fans don't even remember is, in some sense, a waste of time. But when it comes to the politics of pop canonization, institutions such as the Recording Academy and the Rock & Roll Hall of Fame (Mariah has been eligible since 2015 but has yet to be nominated) still hold sway in the writing of our cultural history, perhaps because nothing of comparable authority or prestige has come along to take their place. Mariah is far from the only woman or artist of color to have been neglected. In her book *Liner Notes for the Revolution*, scholar Daphne A. Brooks identifies an egregious pattern: "How is it possible for Black women popular musicians to exist simultaneously at the fringe and yet at the center of the culture industry?"[3] In other words, how can someone as influential as Mariah still be so underappreciated? For those who remember how her artistry was dismissed by tastemakers in the '90s, the belated acclaim she has received can seem like paltry restitution.

Long-standing biases certainly play a role in Mariah's

uneven reception, but so do a string of fumbles and gaffes that have periodically overshadowed her music. A stint on *American Idol* in 2013 — which she later called "the worst experience of my life"[4] — exposed her on live TV at her most stilted and awkward, and embroiled her in an inexplicable, season-long duel with rapper Nicki Minaj. Then in 2016, after a technical glitch at a New Year's Eve performance in Times Square, she was cast as a spoiled prima donna who'd forgotten the meaning of "the show must go on." After several interminable minutes of dead airtime, she huffed off the stage exasperated and defeated, a prerecorded track playing in the background seeming to have revealed her intentions to lip-sync her way through the most challenging parts of her set. It was a cringe-worthy mishap for an artist whose early days were characterized by well-oiled professionalism, and the media and Twittersphere dug their claws in. Later, an indignant Mariah said to an interviewer, "It's like I'm the only one who has to make five million comebacks . . . it's not okay that I was just victimized and vilified by the situation."[5]

Lambs notice when their idol is made the subject of collective mockery, and some take it personally, even when it's clear she's in on the joke. But career hiccups are now essential to her mythos. This is one of the abiding paradoxes of Mariah fandom: even as we long for her to be vindicated, it's also apparent that our ability to believe she's misunderstood and underestimated is what fosters our evangelical zeal. As long as a sizable swath of the public goes on thinking of her as a capricious, undisciplined diva — a remnant of a bygone era of superstardom, resting on her laurels — the lambs can look to the depth and wit of her best music as a secret, a treasure waiting to be uncovered by anyone willing to give her work a close listen.

Most lambs stay loyal not just out of nostalgia but because the new music, when it comes, is remarkably good. Each album Mariah has released since the late aughts has contained some of her finest work. Particularly worthy of reassessment is 2014's eclectic and kookily titled *Me. I Am Mariah . . . The Elusive Chanteuse*, which boasts a handful of the most blissed-out dance tracks she's ever placed on an album. These songs include "Meteorite," a Q-Tip-produced disco stomper built on the chunky percussion of an Eddie Kendricks sample, and "You Don't Know What to Do," which benefits from a sizzling string arrangement by Larry Gold, a former member of Philadelphia International Records' revered house band, MFSB. Alongside these up-tempos are a few accusatory torch songs, my favorite of which is "Camouflage," a lover's lament that could be read as a harbinger of her divorce from Nick Cannon (initiated a few months after the album's release). A master class in vocal arranging, the track features gospel-infused background singing that swells, ebbs, and cradles Mariah at her most dejected-sounding. In its best moments, *Elusive Chanteuse* is shot through with restless energy and urgency; it's the work of an artist who creates as much out of her own needs and desires as for her fans.

When critics take the long view of an artist's discography, it can be tempting to emphasize turning points and quantum leaps at the expense of smaller-scale accomplishments. But what interests me most about this recent stretch in Mariah's career is how quietly and patiently she's tended to her craft. Her ambitions may be more modest these days, but her love for music-making hasn't waned, and it's this steadfastness that has helped her outlast other brilliant singers whose careers have been halted by external distractions, a dearth of good material, or plain and simple exhaustion. For me, Mariah's legacy is not just a tally of the milestones and innovations that defined her first fifteen years in the heat of the spotlight. The fact that the best of her post-*Emancipation* music holds its own next to her biggest '90s hits has little to do with her status as a global icon; instead, it's the mark of a working professional who plies her trade consistently and exceptionally well.

"Candy Bling" is a mid-career masterpiece that plays as if it might have been written in a matter of minutes. The song is featured on Mariah's 2009 release *Memoirs of an Imperfect Angel*, which is notable for containing some of her sharpest jokes and double entendres (listen to the highly quotable "It's a Wrap" and the loony "Up Out My Face" for a taste of how laugh-out-loud funny Mariah's lyrics can get). The album's sound is defined by the elaborate productions of The-Dream and Tricky Stewart, an in-demand duo who were coming off the blockbuster success of Rihanna's "Umbrella" and Beyoncé's "Single Ladies." In contrast, "Candy Bling" sounds like an afterthought, its finger-snap beat seemingly cobbled together on the fly. The song is a reverie about an evanescent love, reminiscent of Mariah's forays into quiet storm in the mid- and late 1990s. But more than a decade after "Underneath the Stars," we're conscious of the distance that separates the narrator from the puppy love she describes. She's older and wiser than she once was, and the sting of loss is no longer fresh. As she itemizes the things she shared with a former beau ("tag, chase, spin the bottle," "anklets, name plates that you gave to me"), you can picture her peering through the mists of time, grasping at objects that have long since become intangible. The chorus — a rewrite of Ahmad's 1994 melodic rap hit "Back in the Day" — swirls like a whirlpool, sucking us into an irretrievable past, as a choir of heavy-breathing Mariahs intone "back, back, back" on the off-beat, like fairies casting a spell. Poised precisely between bitterness and sweetness, "Candy Bling" acknowledges that some losses can never be restored, and that music is a safe place where we can reconcile the fantasy of love with reality. In Mariah's view, it's the yearnings that seem innocuous and the what-ifs that seem juvenile that are the true wellsprings of grown-up pain.

Mariah likes to joke that she doesn't acknowledge time (and true fans know she refuses to celebrate her birthdays, calling them "anniversaries"). But her work contradicts this. The eternal return of "All I Want for Christmas Is You" points to her investment in time — and in the idea that an illusion of constancy can be constructed out of time's cyclical rhythms. "Candy Bling" is similarly obsessed with time's passage, as is a highlight from the terrific 2018 album *Caution*. The song "8th Grade" is her first official outing with Timbaland, a towering figure of turn-of-the-millennium hip-hop and R&B. Both the song's middle-school-invoking title and the period associations of the collaboration suggest a helpless longing for the past, one in which the plenitude of R&B — the sheer abundance of a genre undergoing a culture-shifting renaissance — served as a balm for the heartbreaks of youth. Mariah sings of wanting to be at the center of her prospective dream lover's world, of not knowing where she stands with him, but her tone is leisurely rather than desperate. Where young Mariah would have saturated the track with harmonies and riffs, mature Mariah is content to communicate her romantic intentions in the most straightforward way she can muster.

I've always gravitated toward Mariah's emotional openness — that mixture of power and vulnerability characteristic of so many great R&B singers — but I don't know if the word "wise" has ever come to mind when I think about her music. Listening to "Candy Bling" and "8th Grade," though, I'm struck by how tenderly they evoke a certain kind of knowledge, an acceptance of love as both presence and absence. There's an all-embracing serenity in them that didn't exist in Mariah's early years, when her music was distinguished by overwhelming feelings, usually expressed at fever pitch. From the mixed moods and temporalities of these songs, we might infer a lesson: love may end — or may never even get started — but the music lives on, helping us face our disappointments without resentment or regret. We can survive our unfulfilled longings, and in time, we can learn to look fondly on them. Wistful but relaxed, these songs could have been composed from a horizontal position on a chaise longue, with a glass of wine in hand.

Throughout this book, I've tried to give Mariah's talents as a songwriter, producer, and vocal arranger the attention they deserve — to show that they go far beyond mere competence, that they form the core of her legacy. At the same time, I've wanted to avoid the suggestion that there's more ingenuity to be found at the tip of a pen or at a mixing board than behind a microphone. Mariah's larger-than-life vocal style is the ultimate vehicle for her musical intelligence, and for multiple generations of pop singers around the world, it has stood as a model to be emulated. It calls to mind a theory that writer John Potter poses in his book *Vocal Authority*: throughout the history of Western music, singing styles tend to develop until they achieve dominance, then reach a point of such intricacy that they can only plateau when singers begin to employ their techniques indiscriminately.[6] We might consider Mariah a present-day analog of early-sixteenth-century classical singers, whom Potter describes as the apotheosis of decadent aestheticism. Like theirs, Mariah's vocal style feels like an endpoint in a historical cycle, a mode so maximalist that it's hard to imagine where the art of singing will go next.

Mariah's voice has given rise to a set of values that govern our ideas about good pop and R&B singing today. A near-universal shorthand for vocal virtuosity, her name tends to come up whenever a young female powerhouse hits the scene: this was the case when Christina Aguilera emerged in the late '90s, as well as when Ariana Grande sprinkled whistle notes into her debut album in 2013. Just as notable as Mariah's influence on American singers is her popularity among vocalists overseas, especially in Asia. Sohyang, a dynamic soprano given to displays of melismatic indulgence, has been nicknamed "the Korean Mariah Carey." Jane Zhang — one of the most famous singers to emerge from *Super Girl*, a Chinese TV competition with a viewership of over two billion — is known for the whistle tones ("dolphin tones" in Mandarin) she learned by singing along to Mariah's records as a child. The Philippines, with its vibrant traditions of karaoke and singing competitions, has produced numerous high-profile Mariah acolytes, including the great balladeer Regine Velasquez, who has covered Mariah's songs on national television. When I spoke to Velasquez, she explained how Mariah's popularity opened a market for Filipina divas with booming voices like hers, known as "*birit* queens":

> I grew up joining amateur singing contests, and what you do when you're competing is show off what you can do with your voice. That was my training; that's how I got my style. But that wasn't what was popular in the mid-'80s; Filipinos were more interested in easy listening at the time. That wasn't my vibe. Then Mariah got popular, and I was able to fill a gap in our industry, since no one was doing that particular sound yet. I studied her ad-libs and her runs, and before I knew it, I became obsessed.[7]

As R&B became a musical mainstay across the globe, it redefined ideas about vocal beauty. In 2023, *Rolling Stone* published a list of the greatest singers of all time, and nine of the top ten slots were occupied by R&B vocalists — with Mariah sitting at number five as the highest-ranked living artist. But you don't need an official canon to show you how profound the influence of the genre's distinct vocal culture has been. For decades, the sounds of Black women's singing have been ineluctably appropriated, internationalized, and removed from the specificity of their origins — and for better or worse, the popularity of Mariah's music has been one of the primary vectors along which these developments have unfolded. The age of social media, which has brought forth a spirit of vocal one-upmanship on YouTube, Instagram, and TikTok, has further ensured that the bells and whistles that once distinguished Mariah from her peers are now quite common among Gen-Z amateur singers across racial backgrounds. If you grew up like I did, in an era when the gift of vocal virtuosity was understood to be an exceedingly finite resource, this may come as a surprise. What happens when a rarefied, Olympian style of singing that once existed at the outer limits of human capability becomes so integrated into the fabric of pop culture that it ceases to be exceptional?

Critic Ben Ratliff has observed that "the listener recognizing virtuosity is made naïve, at least for a moment. To respond to music performed at such a high level is to temporarily leave the Earth; it is to take part in a kind of fantasy."[8] A high note flawlessly nailed, a tricky rhythm precisely rendered, a complex and surprising melisma executed with razor-sharp accuracy: these vocal victories can bring a feeling of clarity — of *rightness* — to the havoc of human emotion. Encountering a singer as awe-inspiring as Mariah, listeners are drawn into the sonic dream she weaves, and some partake of it not through passive spectatorship but through active imitation. The distance these listeners feel between themselves and their idol is something like unrequited love. It nags at them; it cries out to be eliminated. The desire to close this gap is part of how the world's supply of virtuosos renews itself.

Up-and-coming singers may be able to convincingly mimic Mariah's skill set, but her sumptuous tone is one pleasure that isn't so easily duplicated. Another is the unique way she thinks and feels with her voice — an ability that remains even as her instrument gets less consistent with the years. You can hear evidence of this in a video of a performance Mariah gave to a group of fans after a taping of *Late Night with Jimmy Fallon*, uploaded to YouTube in 2013. Featuring "Big Jim" Wright on piano, this four-minute moment is pure, unplugged improvisation, and one of the few documents we have of Mariah's voice leading her down new melodic pathways in real time. Her off-the-cuff banter, sung over the chords of her 2005 gospel track "Fly Like a Bird," is by turns loopy and disarmingly funny. We don't know where the jam session is going, and neither does she, but the results remind us that she is a musician for whom voice and mind are one, and for whom singing is as necessary a form of communication as speaking. We get to hear her move through a series of musical challenges and land on solutions, all while making it look as natural and easy as a conversation she's having with friends. Sometimes I wish the rest of her career could be made up of intimate exchanges like this, brief and unfiltered glimpses of her brain at work.

Perhaps the most significant thing that continues to set Mariah apart from the many young singers who have learned to match her note for note, riff for riff, is an idea about salvation — the knowledge that her voice has, at one time or another, stood between the listener and oblivion. As much as romantic commitment, professional ambition, or familial duty, the sound of a voice can be a source of inspiration to keep on living. I can't separate my love for Mariah from the belief that her voice has saved lives, including gay ones like mine. Nowadays, Mariah's deified status within certain corners of the queer community is taken for granted. Her music is a staple of drag shows big and small, and her mere name allows romance to blossom between two men in the popular sitcom *Schitt's Creek*. In recent years, gay writers' accounts of how Mariah's music helped them come to terms with their sexuality have turned up in the *New York Times* and the *Guardian*, furthering the notion of her voice as a path to queer survival.

When I think about the elder pen pal I met on that listserv in the late '90s, I wonder what we might have been trying to say to each other about our lives in all our appraisals of favorite singers, correspondences in which the topics of sexual identity, homophobia, and heartbreak were, as far as I can remember, never once broached. Just as opera and Broadway have served as secret languages within segments of the gay world, I suppose the vernacular of pop and R&B divadom became for the two of us a kind of Morse code. That's why, even now, an encounter with Mariah's music can sometimes feel to me like a rendezvous with the closet, and with the emptiness I needed her voice to fill. In the words of Wayne Koestenbaum: "The grandiosity of operatic utterance is a wild compensation for the listener's silence."[9]

Lately, I've been thinking about a lanky, feminine white boy I met at an academic summer camp in my high school years. He stayed on the floor above me in a small dorm house in North Carolina. One evening, I returned to my room to hear him singing the climax of an R&B-diva ballad, seemingly to himself, his majestic voice as loud as a siren. The walls of the house vibrated when he belted out the Mariah-like high notes. I was immediately jealous of his virtuosity and apparent lack of shame — a confidence bordering on arrogance. Talent and queerness were fused together in my perception of his performance. I regret never telling him how much I admired his singing. I regret never having the nerve to sing as fearlessly.

He didn't seem to have many friends, and I don't think I heard him speak more than a few sentences during the monthlong camp. But I never saw any of our dorm mates, even the preeningly macho ones, give him a hard time. If anything, they kept their distance. A voice like his might not win over hearts and minds, but it can shut people up, stun them into silence. Anticipating his exile from the world, the singer creates his own.

The immateriality of the voice makes it akin to the spirit. In fact, Aristotle defined *voice* as "the sound produced by a creature possessing a soul."

For most of its presence on earth, the voice has been a casualty of history, mortal and undocumented. It's without mass; it weighs nothing. It's a mystery that comes from inside the body, reliant on the coordination of several different muscles and organs, carried out on a current of air before dissipating without a trace. Our identities are wrapped around it — and race, gender, class, and sexual orientation are often inferred from it — but the voice evades tidy classification, because no individual voice sounds exactly like another. Because the voice seems not entirely of this world, untouchable and unplaceable, it can slip between the cracks and penetrate the deepest recesses of ourselves. Is it any wonder that so much sacred ritual, across religions and cultures, hinges on vocalization, or that the Bible is filled with mentions of the voice and the Lord's persistent requests for us to make joyful use of it?

The voice's uncanny power can become domesticated through the ubiquity of pop music. But Mariah's extreme style foregrounds the ways singing can activate something irrational and untamed within us. The improbable regions of her instrument are no less berserk than the most haunting human sounds in the history of recorded music: Screamin' Jay Hawkins's gothic growl, Tom Waits's froggy drawl, Jimmy Scott's androgynous warble, Joanna Newsom's high-pitched squawk. This is singing that seems piped in from another universe — singing that can bring you to your knees.

Even if we were to stop short of leaping into the divine, we might at least try to understand why singers like Mariah are spoken about in such mystical terms. I gave up on religion long ago, but her voice seems to scratch some spiritual itch I still feel inside me, one that I assume will never go away. I'm fascinated by the visceral ways in which people who love virtuosic singing (especially fans of lavishly expressive styles such as R&B, gospel, and opera) react to it, as if in the throes of possession. Some of us feel jolts of pleasure that researchers have called "skin orgasms," psychophysiological reactions partially explained by scientific studies that liken the neurological effect of music to that of sex and drugs.[10] Some of us respond with gestures of ecstasy: closing our eyes, trembling and shuddering, scrunching up our faces, holding our hands up as if to catch the sound in midair. I believe it's possible for a listener to identify so intensely with the singer that he feels her voice vibrating in his throat. A few times I've dreamed of Mariah's voice coming out of my mouth — dreamed of bending sound to my will, like she does — and have woken up in a state of rapture.

Time passes, and I still experience Mariah's singing as an ever-renewing shock to the system. For me, her voice embodies not just a manner of singing but an ethos: she's one of pop's reigning transcendentalists. Like the diva geniuses in whose footsteps she follows, she's serious in her belief that a voice — *her* voice — can put us in communion with the sublime.

# ACKNOWLEDGMENTS

Without the friendship of a few fellow lambs — Lisa Thomas, Sharlene Chiu, Rhea Daniels, and Josephine Llorente — this book wouldn't exist. "If you just believe in me, I will love you endlessly."

I owe so much to my family in the United States, Malaysia, Taiwan, and Australia. A special shout-out goes to my parents; my sister, Adeline; and my cousin Estelle Tang.

It was a pleasure to work with editors Casey Kittrell and Oliver Wang, who took a chance on this project and whose encouragement has been a great help to me.

I'm grateful to Claudrena Harold, Emily Lordi, Isabel Sandoval, Craig Seymour, Danyel Smith, and Regine Velasquez for sharing their time and brilliant insights with me. I'm indebted to lamb extraordinaire Raymond Ang for making a crucial introduction.

Finally, I want to thank a few other people who supported and inspired me throughout the writing process: Melissa Anderson, Franklin Gilliam, Michael Koresky, Benjamin Mercer, Shala Miller, Goeun Minshall, and Jesse Trussell.

# NOTES

## Chapter I: A Call to Worship

1. Caroline A. Streeter, *Tragic No More: Mixed-Race Women and the Nexus of Sex and Celebrity* (Amherst: University of Massachusetts Press, 2012), 65–66.
2. Sasha Frere-Jones, "On Top," *New Yorker*, April 3, 2006.
3. Ryan Schocket, "22 Times Mariah Carey Was Absolutely Not Human At All," *Buzzfeed*, February 21, 2022, buzzfeed.com/ryanschocket2/mariah -carey-is-a-superhuman.
4. Meredith Monk, "Notes on the Voice," *Painted Bride Quarterly* 3, No. 2 (1976), 13–14.
5. Wayne Koestenbaum, *The Queen's Throat* (New York: Da Capo Press, 1993), 3.

## Chapter 2: What a Voice Means

1. Tommy Mottola, with Cal Fussman, *Hitmaker: The Man and His Music* (New York: Grand Central Publishing, 2013), 182.
2. Classic Mariah Archive, "Mariah Carey — Vision of a Daydream Interview," YouTube, youtube.com/watch?v=ySwtM1XuMxk.
3. Mariah Carey, with Michaela Angela Davis, *The Meaning of Mariah Carey* (New York: Andy Cohen Books, 2020), 6.
4. Carey, *The Meaning of Mariah Carey*, 52.
5. Mottola, *Hitmaker*, 185.
6. Carey, *The Meaning of Mariah Carey*, 215.
7. Mottola, *Hitmaker*, 279.
8. Carey, *The Meaning of Mariah Carey*, 121.
9. Fred Goodman, "The Marketing Muscle Behind Mariah Carey," *New York Times*, April 14, 1991, nytimes.com/1991/04/14/arts/pop-music-the -marketing-muscle-behind-mariah-carey.html.
10. Robert Sam Anson, "Tommy Boy," *Vanity Fair*, December 1996, archive .vanityfair.com/article/1996/12/tommy-boy.

11. Vixen, "Mariah Carey Hires Jermaine Dupri as Manager," *Vibe*, October 7, 2013: vibe.com/features/vixen/mariah-carey-hires-jermaine-dupri-as -manager-289101.

12. Mottola, *Hitmaker*, 214.

13. David Metzer, "The Power Ballad," *Popular Music*, Vol. 31, No. 3 (October 2012).

14. Carey, *The Meaning of Mariah Carey*, 141.

15. Mottola, *Hitmaker*, 246.

## Chapter 3: Other Sounds, Other Realms

1. Kelsey McKinney, "A Hit Song Is Usually 3 to 5 Minutes Long. Here's Why," Vox, January 30, 2015, vox.com/2014/8/18/6003271/why-are-songs -3-minutes-long.

2. Gary Burns, "A Typology of 'Hooks' in Popular Records," *Popular Music*, Vol. 6, No. 1 (January 1987), 1–20.

3. Finn Johannsen, "David Morales: Living to Just Play Music," Groove, September 20, 2016, groove.de/2016/09/20/david-morales-def-mix -interview-finn-johannsen/3.

4. Craig Seymour, author interview, phone, May 28, 2021.

5. IMR Radio, "Tim Lawrence Interview—David Mancuso & the Loft heritage," YouTube, October 4, 2019, youtube.com/watch?v= Uhb2VzsK2AU.

6. Barry Laine, "Disco Dancing: Too Hot for Love," *Christopher Street*, June 1978.

7. Mariah Carey, with Michaela Angela Davis, *The Meaning of Mariah Carey* (New York: Andy Cohen Books, 2020), 139.

8. Claudrena Harold, author interview, phone, January 17, 2022. For a thorough and brilliant overview of contemporary gospel, read Harold's book *When Sunday Comes: Gospel Music in the Soul and Hip-Hop Eras* (Champaign: University of Illinois Press, 2020).

9. Carey and Davis, *The Meaning of Mariah Carey*, 51.

10. Michael Eric Dyson, "Black or White? Labels Don't Always Fit," *New York Times*, February 13, 1994.

## Chapter 4: Out of the Chrysalis

1. Christopher John Farley, "Pop's Princess Grows Up," *Time*, September 25, 1995.

2. Andrew Mueller, "Mariah Carey, *Mariah Carey* (CBS)," *Melody Maker*, 15, Spring 1990.

3. Brittany Luse, "Mariah Carey and the Fiction of the Color Line," Vulture, October 18, 2021, vulture.com/article/mariah-carey-nella-larsen-passing .html.

4. Lisa Jones, *Bulletproof Diva* (New York: Anchor Books, 1994), 201.

5. Mariahxlambily, "Mariah Carey on Why She Hates Singing on TV & Reflects on 1990 'America the Beautiful' Vocals!," YouTube, youtube.com/watch?v=zFwx_nviMs8.

6. Mariah Carey, with Michaela Angela Davis, *The Meaning of Mariah Carey* (New York: Andy Cohen Books, 2020), 222.

7. Elysa Gardner, "Cinderella Story," *Vibe*, April 1996.

8. Gardner, "Cinderella Story."

9. Quoted in David Brackett, *Categorizing Sound: Genre and Twentieth-Century Popular Music* (Oakland: University of California Press, 2016), 245.

10. Kelefa Sanneh, *Major Labels: A History of Popular Music in Seven Genres* (New York: Penguin Press, 2021), 152.

11. Fuse, "Mariah Carey | On The Record | Fuse," YouTube, January 24, 2017, youtube.com/watch?v=flIIZaIQXBE.

12. Carey, *The Meaning of Mariah Carey*, 175.

13. Carey, *The Meaning of Mariah Carey*, 97.

14. "Rap Records: Are They Fad or Permanent?" *Billboard*, February 16, 1980, 57.

15. Tricia Rose, *The Hip Hop Wars: What We Talk About When We Talk About Hip Hop—and Why It Matters* (New York: Basic Books, 2008), 8.

16. Dan Charnas, *The Big Payback: The History of the Business of Hip-Hop* (New York: New American Library, 2010).

17. Carey, *The Meaning of Mariah Carey*, 210.

18. Carey, *The Meaning of Mariah Carey*, 198.

19. Carey, *The Meaning of Mariah Carey*, 100.

20. "Mariah Carey Tells All! Untold 'Butterfly' Tales, Her Biopic Series, New Music, and Much More," *Rolling Stone Music Now*, September 16, 2022.

## Chapter 5: Between Laughter and Lament

1. Cole Delbyck, "Mariah Carey Celebrates Her 50th Birthday, Insists She's 'Eternally 12,'" *Huffington Post*, March 29, 2020, huffpost.com/entry /mariah-carey-50th-birthday-eternally-12_n_5e80de2cc5b6cb9dc1a22a1d.

2. Mariah Carey, with Michaela Angela Davis, *The Meaning of Mariah Carey* (New York: Andy Cohen Books, 2020), 221.

3. Brittany Spanos, "Mariah Carey's Former Engineer Details Secret Alt-Rock Album Recording," *Rolling Stone*, October 5, 2020, rollingstone.com /music/music-features/mariah-carey-chick-album-engineer-1070305.

4. Matthew Jacobs, "The Never-ending Story of *Glitter*, 20 Years On," Vulture, September 11, 2021, vulture.com/2021/09/the-never-ending -story-of-glitter-20-years-on.html.

5. OWN, "Mariah Carey: 'Nobody Could Fully Understand My Experience,'" YouTube, August 6, 2020, youtube.com/watch?v=Pcz_72_8a58.

6. Elizabeth Hardwick, *Sleepless Nights* (New York: New York Review of Books, 2001), 26.

7. Richard Dyer, *Heavenly Bodies: Film Stars and Society* (London: Routledge, 1986), 145.

8. THE HD LAMBILY, "BBMAs Artist of The Decade - Mariah Carey Speech," YouTube, June 30, 2021, youtube.com/watch?v=2JTTIxTukCo.

9. Carey, *The Meaning of Mariah Carey*, 219.

10. Elysa Gardner, "Cinderella Story," *Vibe*, April 1996.

11. Carey, *The Meaning of Mariah Carey*, 73.

12. Greil Marcus, *Mystery Train: Images of America in Rock 'n' Roll Music* (New York: Penguin, 1975), 127.

13. Justice for Mariah, "Mariah Carey's surprise Appearance on Total Request Live MTV 2001," YouTube, July 31, 2020, youtube.com/watch?v=J2smQ6LcR8I.

14. Carey, *The Meaning of Mariah Carey*, 239.

15. Carey, *The Meaning of Mariah Carey*, 253.

16. Carey, *The Meaning of Mariah Carey*, 237.

17. "Mariah—Back Facing the Music," NBC News, December 3, 2002, nbcnews.com/id/wbna3080087.

18. Lawrence Van Gelder, "Dreaming a Dream and Paying the Price for It," *New York Times*, September 21, 2001, nytimes.com/2001/09/21/movies/film-review-dreaming-a-dream-and-paying-the-price-for-it.html.

19. Nicole Seymour, *Glitter* (New York: Bloomsbury Academic, 2022), 12.

20. Michael Atkinson, "Eat Drink Man Mariah," *Village Voice*, September 25, 2001, villagevoice.com/2001/09/25/eat-drink-man-mariah.

21. James Baldwin, *The Devil Finds Work* (New York: Vintage, 1976), 30.

## Chapter 6: Back at Number I

1. Mariahxlambily, "RARE: Mariah Carey Talks/Analyses Her Voice In-Depth! (1999)," YouTube, November 2, 2018, youtube.com/watch?v=QH6wC7zrRK0.

2. TERRELL, "KELLY PRICE Sings Whitney Houston, Talks Being Fat-Shamed, & Biggest Lessons Mariah Carey Taught Her," YouTube, July 22, 2021, youtube.com/watch?v=qCanZc8bUY8.

3. Mariah Carey Multimedia, "MTV Greatest Voices," YouTube, February 3, 2018, youtube.com/watch?v=8oVG3YKTlvM.

4. MLCQuotes, "Mariah Carey Live on Larry King. (4/5)," YouTube, November 6, 2009, youtube.com/watch?v=inLUHZUn-uE.

5. Da'Shan Smith, "K. Michelle on Being a Monster: 'We Have Different Faces for Different People,'" *Vibe*, February 14, 2020, vibe.com/music/music-news/k-michelle-on-being-a-monster-we-have-different-faces-for-different-people-674685.

6. David Lehmann, "Why 'The Emancipation of Mimi' Made Mariah Carey a Star for the 2000s," Noisey, April 24, 2015, vice.com/en/article/rpyp9m /mariah-carey-the-emancipation-of-mimi-ten-year-anniversary.

7. Lehmann, "Why 'The Emancipation of Mimi' Made Mariah Carey a Star for the 2000s."

8. Jermaine Dupri, with Samantha Marshall, *Young, Rich, and Dangerous: The Making of a Music Mogul* (New York: Atria Books, 2007), 242.

9. Ted Gioia, *Love Songs: The Hidden History* (Oxford: Oxford University Press, 2015), 45.

10. Princess Gabbara, "Mariah Carey on Why 2005's Iconic 'The Emancipation of Mimi' LP Was 'More Than a Comeback Album,'" *Billboard*, April 10, 2020, billboard.com/music/pop/mariah-carey -interview-the-emancipation-of-mimi-anniversary-9356111.

## Chapter 7: A Timeless Diva through Time

1. Jenn Pelly, "Grimes Speaks Out in Defense of Beyoncé, 'Gangnam Style,' and Mariah Carey," *Pitchfork*, February 6, 2013, pitchfork.com/news /49448-grimes-speaks-out-in-defense-of-beyonce-gangnam-style-and -mariah-carey.

2. Danyel Smith, *Shine Bright: A Very Personal History of Black Women in Pop* (New York: Roc Lit 101, 2022), 256.

3. Daphne A. Brooks, *Liner Notes for the Revolution* (Cambridge: Harvard University Press, 2021), 43.

4. Natalie Stone, "Mariah Carey Says 'American Idol' Was 'Worst Experience of My Life,'" *Billboard*, May 28, 2015, billboard.com/music/pop/mariah -carey-says-american-idol-was-the-worst-experience-of-my-6582898.

5. Associated Press, "Carey Says She Was 'Victimized' over NYE Show," YouTube, February 17, 2017, youtube.com/watch?v=Pfd_mIxgPCg.

6. John Potter, *Vocal Authority: Singing Style and Ideology* (Cambridge: Cambridge University Press, 1998), 51.

7. Regine Velasquez, author interview, phone, August 31, 2022.

8. Ben Ratliff, "Mere Virtuosity: Variations on a Slippery Idea," *Virginia Quarterly Review*, Spring 2018, Volume 94, #1.

9. Wayne Koestenbaum, *The Queen's Throat* (New York: Da Capo Press, 1993), 16.

10. David Robson, "The Strange Phenomenon of Musical 'Skin Orgasms,'" *BBC*, July 22, 2015, bbc.com/future/article/20150721-when-was-the-last -time-music-gave-you-a-skin-orgasm.